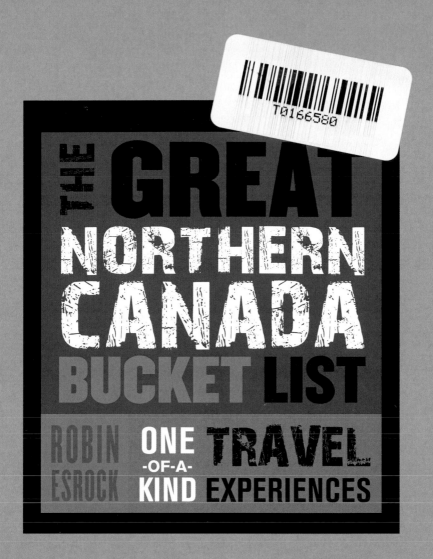

THE GREAT NORTHERN CANADA BUCKET LIST

ROBIN ESROCK

ONE -OF-A- KIND TRAVEL EXPERIENCES

DUNDURN
TORONTO

For Rock, and the good people of the North

Library and Archives Canada Cataloguing in Publication
Esrock, Robin, 1974-, author

The great northern Canada bucket list : one-of-a-kind travel experiences / Robin Esrock.

Issued in print and electronic formats.
ISBN 978-1-4597-3052-6 (paperback).--ISBN 978-1-4597-3053-3 (pdf).
--ISBN 978-1-4597-3054-0 (epub)

1. Esrock, Robin, 1974- --Travel--Canada, Northern. 2. Canada, Northern--Description and travel.
3. Canada, Northern--Guidebooks.I. Title.

FC3954.E86 2016   917.1904'4   C2015-908319-2
                                             C2015-908320-6

Editor: Allison Hirst
Cover and text concept: Tania Craan
Cover design: Courtney Horner
Text design: Laura Boyle
Front cover images: Nansen Weber/Arctic Watch; Robin Esrock; Jeff Topham; Courtesy Government of Yukon/Fritz Mueller; Ruslan Margolin
Back cover images: (centre) Robin Esrock; author photo, Jeff Topham
Printer: Friesens

1   2   3   4   5   20   19   18   17   16

We acknowledge the support of the **Canada Council for the Arts** and the **Ontario Arts Council** for our publishing program. We also acknowledge the financial support of the **Government of Canada** through the **Canada Book Fund** and **Livres Canada Books**, and the **Government of Ontario** through the **Ontario Book Publishing Tax Credit** and the **Ontario Media Development Corporation**.

Printed and bound in Canada.

Visit us at
Dundurn.com | @dundurnpress | Facebook.com/dundurnpress | Pinterest.com/dundurnpress

Dundurn
3 Church Street, Suite 500
Toronto, Ontario, Canada
M5E 1M2

CONTENTS

INTRODUCTION

bucket list: *A list of things one hopes to accomplish in one's lifetime.*

Born and raised in South Africa, it was never too difficult for me to head North. Europe, America, Asia — it was all North to me. As a travel writer and TV host, I've now journeyed to over one hundred countries on seven continents — north, south, east, and west — with such feverish dedication to the cardinal points that I even got a compass tattooed on my leg. But it was only when I spent several years visiting every province and territory in a country often referred to as The Great White North, that I began to grasp exactly what the North actually symbolizes: remote and stark, yet full of life, culture, and adventure. It's also vast. Nunavut alone is bigger than the three largest contiguous U.S. states — California, Montana, and Texas — combined. The population of those three states is seventy-four million. The population of Nunavut is just thirty-six thousand, occupying 20 percent of Canada's landmass (that's bigger than Western Europe or Mexico). Wood Buffalo National Park, which covers parts of the Northwest Territories and Alberta, is almost twice as large as the European nation of Macedonia — not to be confused with *macadamia*, a type of nut, which is what you become if you try and make sense of just how big Canada's North is.

Look, I've spent the past decade scouring the planet for the most mind-blowing, one-of-a-kind experiences I could find. I've been there, done that, and traded the T-shirt for much more impressive souvenirs — like a king scorpion clock and a kangaroo scrotum bottle opener, neither of which my wife will allow in the house. With all this experience, I simply did not expect the North to offer so much adventure, culture, and beauty, all of it unlike anywhere else in the world. Like many southerners, I simply had no idea. After numerous

trips in all seasons, I firmly believe you can't understand Canada unless you experience something of the true North (strong and free). Once you do, you'll quickly understand why our three great northern territories belong on every Canadian's and visitor's bucket list.

When our ancestors looked up at the stars, the heavens were so limitless they became known, quite simply, as space. While it's unlikely we'll travel the depths of the universal cosmos, we can experience space right here on Earth. Instead of Jupiter, Venus, and the worst name for a planet ever, Uranus, we can substitute Yukon, Northwest Territories, and Nunavut, with the satisfaction of knowing these worlds are not only accessible, they're waiting for us. As space tourists on Earth, we're going to need a different set of spaceships to explore these new worlds. An Arctic expedition ship, for example, is the most comfortable way to discover glaciers, fjords, shark fin peaks, and the rolling tundra of the North's great national parks.

In the Yukon, we'll hop aboard a different type of spaceship, leaving the ocean for the skies. Without any roads, the scale of Kluane National Park's ice fields, glaciers, mountains, and valleys can truly be appreciated by air. After all, 82 percent of this massive national park is composed of rock and ice. A flightseeing glacier tour from Haines Junction is not only accessible and surprisingly affordable, but it allows you spot wildlife, turquoise braided streams, the world's largest non-polar ice caps, and Mount Logan, Canada's highest mountain, which has the largest circumference of any non-volcanic mountain on Earth. Flightseeing over NWT's

Mackenzie Delta is just as staggering, while aviation (and television) buffs will no doubt enjoy sitting back in the DC-3 on Buffalo Airway's only scheduled flight.

Our spaceship now needs wheels (and a pair of spares) to take on one of the great road trips in Canada, the Dempster Highway. We'll drive along other meandering highways in search of quirky experiences, abundant wildlife, tasty delights, and unique natural attractions. There are no roads at the world's most northerly eco-lodge, but there are thousands of beluga whales. Wherever we go, there's a distinct thrill at encountering the rare but mythical creatures of the North: muskox, Arctic fox, ptarmigans, caribou, narwhal, and, of course, the polar bear.

Our spaceship must transform into an inflatable boat, capable of withstanding the wildest rapids for one of the world's great river adventures. Rafting inside Nahanni National Park Reserve begins at Virginia Falls, which is only, oh … twice the size of Niagara Falls. Float down twisting waterways between mile-high canyons, evergreen forests, and untouched boreal wilderness. Zodiacs will circle whales and deposit us on remote islands in the mythical Northwest Passage, but reassuringly we can return to the comforts of an expedition mother ship to learn more about Arctic explorers, mysteries, and wildlife. Modern expedition vessels allow us to trace the footsteps of doomed voyages in safety and comfort. When I arrived in the Arctic summer for the first time, I couldn't wait to see the stars at night. We were so isolated, so far away from any light pollution. Well, the stars don't come out because the midnight sun wheels around the horizon. Feeling the sunshine on your skin at two in the morning … that's priceless. First tip of many: when you visit the North in the summer, bring an eye mask.

Yes, summers are understandably more welcoming, but winter brings the glow of our celestial dreams: the northern lights, shimmering above the ice, attracting our imagination like moths to a bonfire. Winter brings extreme cold, but along with it are bucket list activities like dogsledding, ice fishing, and snowmobiling. There are also no mosquitoes, which I felt deserved their own chapter.

Although the North might seem impossibly remote, people have been living in this region for as many as thirty thousand years. Infused in any Arctic experience are their ancestors, the Inuit and Inuvialuit. When you visit this space, you are welcome guests in their space, too. Many visitors are as taken with the cultural exchange in places like Pond Inlet and Inuvik as they are with the landscape. Canada's northern communities are thriving, with healthy traditions paying respect to the environment in which they live. Feast on expensive Arctic char in Yellowknife, but understand the significance, and the experience, of swallowing *muktuk*.

The bucket list appears to be an idea that's time has come. It only surfaced in 2007 when the movie of the same name finally labelled an emotion most of us are very familiar with: the deep longing of wanting to see or do something before we kick our proverbial bucket. Spanning adventure, nature, food, culture, and quirky categories, each item had to tick my own subjective boxes first:

- Is it unique in the world?
- Is it grounded in reality, so that everyone can actually do it?
- Is it something one will remember for the rest of one's life?
- Will it make a great story at a dinner party?

Each experience in this book complies with the above, and then some. Although you may have found this book in the travel section, you'll quickly realize it's not a traditional guidebook. Rather than focusing on accommodation and meal recommendations — many of which might change before this book even goes to print — I've focused on why you should visit these destinations in the first place. It is a personal journey, rife with context and characters, humour, and history. Suitably inspired, I want you to follow in my footsteps in order to create your own adventure. That's why I've created a comprehensive website with all the information you'll need to get started. At the end of each chapter, follow the website link to find practical information, links, meal and accommodation recommendations, videos, galleries, maps, and suggested reading guides. You'll also find regular blog updates, tips, and commentary, and a chance to share your own experiences. Up-to-date information might be great online, but inspiration has always worked wonders on the printed (or digital) page.

Space in Canada's North can be overwhelming. Experience the absence of crowds and noise and malls and traffic and road rage and … exhale. Travelling our northern territories is the sound of your soul taking a deep breath: the quiet, the serenity, the wildlife, the people, the rock, ice, and starkness of tundra. With each escape into this alien world, one feels the goose bumps of pure freedom, where the beauty is so striking and so primal, it's not just the cold tearing up your eyes. My many travels have told me that the harder you work for an experience, the more you appreciate it. That even on rolling tundra, people who surround us shape the experience we enjoy. That a true bucket list experience is one that cannot be replicated anywhere else, and one that you will never forget for as long as you live. Wherever you find yourself looking up at the stars, I hope this book reminds you that earthly spaceships make even the most remote destinations accessible, and that the most remote destinations are often the most magical.

Robin Esrock
Vancouver, B.C.

*Northern Canada can refer to northern regions in Canadian provinces as well as the country's northern territories. Since I have explored the provinces in other Bucket List titles, this book focuses solely on Yukon, the Northwest Territories, and Nunavut.

HOW TO USE THIS BOOK

You will notice this bucket list includes little information about prices, where to stay, where to eat, the best time to go, and what you should pack. Important stuff, but these are practicalities that shift and change with far more regularity than print editions of a book. With this in mind, I've created online and social media channels to accompany the *inspirational* guide you hold in your hands. Here you will find *practical* information, along with videos, galleries, reading suggestions, and more.

By visiting **www.canadianbucketlist.com**, you can also join our community of Bucket Listers, with exclusive discounts to many of the activities featured in this book, automatic entry to win experiences featured in the book, as well as Facebook forums to debate the merits of these, and new adventures. When you register, you can unlock the entire site by entering the code **BUCK3TL15T** and navigating through the provinces, or access each item individually with the **START HERE** link at the end of each chapter.

DISCLAIMER

Tourism is a constantly changing business. Hotels may change names, restaurants may change owners, and some activities may no longer be available at all. Records fall and facts shift. While the utmost care has been taken to ensure the information provided is accurate, the author and publisher take no responsibility for errors, or for any incidents that might occur in your pursuit of these activities.

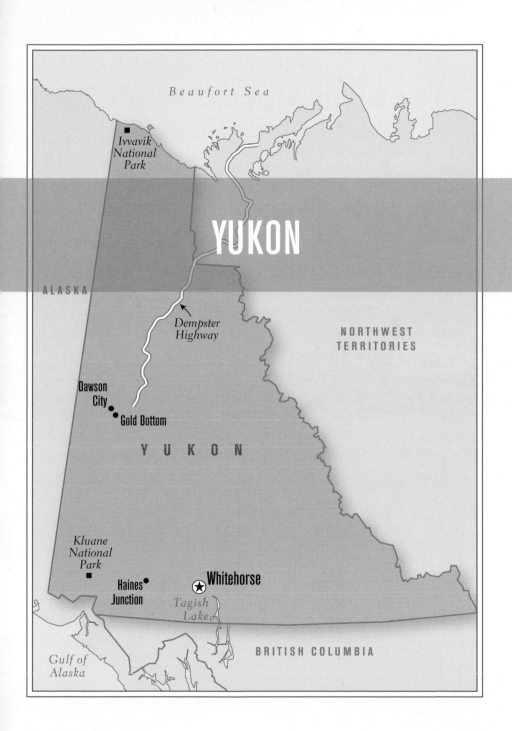

Beaufort Sea

Ivvavik
National
Park

YUKON

ALASKA

Dempster
Highway

NORTHWEST
TERRITORIES

Dawson
City
Gold Bottom

Y U K O N

Kluane
National
Park

Haines
Junction

Whitehorse

Tagish
Lake

Gulf of
Alaska

BRITISH COLUMBIA

DOGSLED WITH A LEGEND

Whitehorse is south of the Arctic Circle, so there is no Arctic night in late November. Still, the Yukon's capital gets light around nine a.m., dark around three p.m., and in between it's too damn cold to be outdoors anyway — unless you've arrived to go dog-sledding, in which case you'll want to drive twenty minutes outside of town to Frank Turner's Muktuk Kennels.

Although he's originally from Toronto, Frank is a venerable dog-sledding legend in the Yukon. He's the only man to have competed in twenty-three consecutive Yukon Quests, known as the "toughest race on earth," routinely placing in the top six, winning it once, and twice receiving the Vets' Choice Award for his exceptional treatment of his dogs. He's the only Canadian-born person to have won the race in three decades, and he held the record for the fastest time record for more than a decade. Joining him for an afternoon dogsled is like having a pond hockey lesson with Wayne Gretzky.

As a dogsledding virgin, I was intrigued, concerned, and ignorant about the concept of harnessing dogs to pull a heavy sled across frozen tundra. When you grow up with apartment dogs, it's difficult to believe that certain breeds thrive in such extreme environments. It instantly became clear that Frank's 125 dogs are treated with as much respect as, if not more than, any suburban poodle — fed the latest naturopathic food, regularly

exercised, and treasured like members of a large, mostly canine family. Each Muktuk dog is lovingly named, given a kennel, and cared for by the staff of international volunteers.

The dogs greet me with enthusiastic howls when I arrive, shaking off the cold, a low sun still pinking up the sky. The dogs circle their kennels amidst a cacophony of barking, making for an exciting welcome. Puppies race excitedly in a large, enclosed, wooden hamster wheel. Muktuk doesn't breed and sell its dogs, and they're made up of various crosses between husky, malamute, wolf, Labrador and tough-as-bones Yukon mutt. Turner frequently takes in local dogs that are in need of a better home, and runs an adoption program for retired sled dogs, but you have to prove yourself a worthy owner first. I inquire how an outdoor sled dog fits into an indoor family home. "Go ahead and ask one," he tells me.

Each dog has its name proudly stencilled on its individual green kennel. I hesitantly approach a husky named Falcon, and am surprised to find him as friendly and good-natured as a golden retriever. Most of them are. Turner is confident any one of his dogs would make a loyal, well-trained pet, and treats them as such.

It's time to suit up in the layers of warm gear provided, including military-style snow boots to keep my feet warm and dry. We're heading out to a frozen river in the Takhini Valley, and I'm commandeered by the team, collecting dogs from their kennels and carrying them to a customized trailer. Turner drops nuggets of advice as we do so. "It's all about teamwork. People think it's the rider in control, but it's all about the dogs. They need to trust you. If the dogs aren't happy, you're not going anywhere." It becomes apparent that despite the spectacular surroundings and the thrill of the sport, dogsledding is more about relationships than anything else.

After a short drive, we arrive at a frozen lake. My eyes become moist, which is not ideal when the temperature is below −30°C. Once unloaded, the dogs eagerly anticipate their run. Frank gives me a brief lesson in dogsledding mechanics: yell "Gee!" for right,

ON THE BUCKET LIST: Frank Turner

I'd love to go to Newfoundland. My image is that it's beautiful, with small communities I can identify with, full of colourful characters. There are some similarities with the Yukon in terms of distance, and I imagine we'd both be considered different from the mainstream.

Frank Turner
Owner, Muktuk Kennels
Yukon Quest Winner

"Haa!" for left and "Whoa whoa!" to stop. Sleds have brakes and foot-pads to control speed. I have six dogs harnessed to my sled, and, as the saying goes, unless you're the lead dog, the view is all the same.

With a whiplash jerk, the dogs set off into the snow, relishing this opportunity to release their pent-up energy. Dog power is not horsepower. Without my control, my team would run themselves senseless, exhausting their energy and possibly injuring themselves. Frank has to constantly remind me to apply the brake, to find the rhythm and flow. Once I do, the true nature of dogsledding — team-work — becomes as clear as the ice crystals clinging to the trees. Watching the effort of each dog, muscles pounding beneath thick fur, how their individual personalities influence their speed and endurance, makes me appreciate how little effort I need to expend to glide across the lake. With the dogs in their groove, I can look up and truly absorb the jaw-dropping scenery around me.

We spend a couple of hours racing along the snow and ice, and I get accustomed to my team, their personalities, their strengths. Val is a firecracker, Livingston a loyal, steadying force. Incredibly, a healthy Quest pack can travel around 160 kilometres a day, at a speed

of around 15 to 20 kilometres per hour, depending on conditions. I imagine Frank's race experiences, wrapped up freezing in the sled as temperatures drop to as low as −70°C, under the bright stars and glowing northern lights. He trains hard all year to prepare his body for the sleep deprivation and physical pounding of the Quest. The unprepared leader puts the team at risk, and the team comes first.

Before the sun sets, we return to the trailers, feed the dogs, and crack out the hot chocolate and thermal warmers, elatedly retreating to Muktuk before the dark afternoon shadows flash-freeze our bones. With a new appreciation for life in the North, you'll be hard pressed to find happier animals — people or dogs — than on a dog-sled adventure.

START HERE: canadianbucketlist.com/dogsled

CAMP IN THE HIGH ARCTIC

"Hypothetically speaking, who would you pick in a death battle — a grizzly versus a gorilla? What about a wolverine up against a Tasmanian devil?" I'm asking these questions of my increasingly bemused hiking group as we continue our trek along the alpine ridges to a lookout called "Halfway to Heaven." Wolverines are on my brain, because we'd just seen one scrambling across the mountainside, an event that solicited tremendous excitement. This is because nobody has ever actually *seen* a wolverine before, not even Terry, an Albertan who has worked in forestry for twenty-five years. Terry owns a company called Wolverine IRM.

"I don't even know a single person who has ever actually seen one," he tells us elatedly, "except you guys!" Judging by the reaction of our group, one would think we'd have had a better chance of

YUKON

spotting Hugh Jackman brandishing titanium claws above the Arctic poppies. This is but one example of the moments that inspire visits to Canada's North, and in particular, Ivvavik National Park.

Every year, more people summit Mount Everest than visit Ivvavik National Park. Located in northern Yukon, although accessed via the western territorial centre of Inuvik (see page 56), Ivvavik stretches sixteen thousand square kilometres across a region protected as the calving grounds of the porcupine caribou (Ivvavik translates as "a place for giving birth" in Inuvialuit). It is also the first national park in Canada created through an Aboriginal land claim agreement. As remote as it is, I am surprised to learn we will not be camping in pristine, untouched wilderness, but rather in the remains of an abandoned gold mining camp. What's more, my vision of seeing more than one hundred thousand caribou mowing tundra in one of the planet's great animal migrations was not realistic, as the caribou migrate in June, and due to unpredictable weather, Parks Canada only offers hosted visits during the month of July. It's a relatively new direction for this vital national agency, enticing hikers with hot showers, flush toilets, hot cooked meals, and on-site cultural guides and naturalist interpreters. Still, fewer than two hundred people will make the journey each summer, because we *are* talking about the remote western Arctic, which is neither cheap nor easy to access. But when you do, well … we'll get to that.

Flying in the North can be touch and go. I missed my chance to visit Torngat Mountain National Park in northern Labrador because of foul weather. If it's not the weather, it might be smoke from summer wildfires, creating a sepia-toned Martian sky. I was, therefore, delighted that Aklak Air's Twin Otter made it into the sky, and even more so that the low-altitude flight over the magnificent Mackenzie Delta turned out to be one of the most stunning flights of my career. Waterways cut in every direction, occasionally marked by traditional whaling and fishing camps. I see a moose and some tundra swans, but most of all, I see a landscape so strikingly different from any I've seen before. Our Parks Canada interpreter, Cassandra, has an E.B. White quote on her bag. It reads, rather serendipitously: "Always be on the lookout for wonder."

We make three passes over the runway. Sheep Creek "International Airport" is little more than a patch of open space, and we land with a jolt on the rocky track. Swapping out with the previous week's guests, they all assure us we're in for a treat. Our group consists of seven hikers, two park interpreters, and an indigenous escort, with two cooks already at base camp. Among us are a retired couple from Whitehorse, a newly married couple from Alberta, an ER nurse from Halifax, and a doctor from Edmonton, prompting a visible sigh of relief to have lucked out with our very own medical unit. We will come to know one another very well in the next four days. There will be long conversations about the environment, trail songs, and feisty games of cribbage. Meals with "Scotch" coffee, traditional Inuit sewing lessons, patio yarns, and short walks to the swimming hole. The camp is encircled by a protective electric bear fence, which admittedly takes the edge off, although the fence does little to stop the real menace of the region: the mosquitoes.

Female mosquitoes need blood to nourish their eggs. In the one week or so they're alive, these insects lay up to five hundred eggs, and in the short Arctic summer, mosquitoes get very hungry indeed. This circle of life comes to an abrupt end with each mosquito I crush with the palm of my hand. *Splat! Splat! Splat!* Most Canadian outdoor adventures are accompanied by biting insects, though they seldom show up in the tourism brochures. You also won't read much about horseflies, which the locals in Inuvik call bulldogs, flying about as they do with the menace of a predator drone. There's a dream catcher in the window, and I find myself thinking about a dream catcher/bug zapper combo, until a mosquito lands on my wrist. "In South Africa, we would call this a hummingbird," I tell the group, squashing the bug with my other palm, "although our hummingbirds aren't vampires."

"There's still gold in this creek," says Don, a retired geologist from Whitehorse. He's enthusiastically furnishing details about the land we find ourselves in, a land that rather uniquely was not glaciated during the last ice age. Evidence of this is found in the unique banks

The DEW Line

of the gemstone Firth River, and the rocky *tors* that crest surrounding alpine ridges like plates on a stegosaurus. Beneath a midnight sun that burns through the smoke blowing in from the Alaskan wildfires, the taiga blushes with purple wild crocus, yellow poppies, and Arctic cotton. Not too hot and not too cold makes for fine hiking weather, and as the only humans to be found in about 94,500 protected square kilometres (including the adjacent Vuntut National Park and Arctic National Wildlife Refuge) our foot-bound mode of transport reveals to us but a fraction of the area. Hikers in Ivvavik primarily stick to the area around base camp at Sheep's Creek. With four days on the ground, we will tackle four outstanding day hikes.

It's a relief to scramble over the bumpy tussocks up into the hills, escaping the willow and sagebrush to bask in bug-free streams of mountain wind. It makes the longest hike, to Wolf Tors, all the more enjoyable as we eat sandwiches at Inspiration Point with the world at our feet. There are wolves in the area (caught on the motion-sensor camera located just outside of our camp), but the view from this rocky outcrop has me howling across the valley. We arrive back in camp with throbbing feet and a healthy appetite for Louisa's home-made bread, bannock, and barbecued chicken.

Having grown up with lions and zebras, I'm not what one would call "bear-aware." This is my first experience with bear bangers, bear spray, and understanding bear behaviour. If the bear is attacking, run … don't play dead … make yourself look bigger … but don't forget to cower! I'm told of one clueless European visitor who actually fumigated his tent with bear spray. On our hike to Inspiration Point, a large adult grizzly heads our way just outside of camp. I'm too stricken to reach for my camera. Ambling upwind, it finally notices our group, and bolts in the opposite direction.

"That's how most bear encounters go," explains our Parks guide, Nelson. But you never know. Past the disintegrating remains of a trapper camp, Terry pulls out his fishing rod while the group dozes off on the gravel alongside the turquoise Firth River. Satiated on sandwiches, protected by my bug net, and exhausted from the hike, I doze into a dreamy state, awakened by the yells of "I've got one!" as Terry hauls in a four-kilogram Dolly Varden, the largest fish Nelson has ever seen pulled from the river, especially at this time of year. "That's one beautiful fish," he says admiringly.

It put up a great fight, and it will make a great dinner once it's hauled back to Louisa's kitchen. In the world of fishing, this is as good as it gets.

"That's the highlight of his trip," remarks his wife, Cyara. Terry is beaming.

Fittingly, our final hike falls on Canada Day. "Halfway to Heaven" kicks off with a steep ascent up the ridge behind base camp, traversing along several ridges (there's the wolverine!) until it reaches a lime-stone peak with rock windows that face out over the valley, over the layered hills that fade into the lavender haze. It's a bucket list moment, further accentuated by the sheer amount of effort it took to reach this spot, and the knowledge that so few others have been here before us.

The vast amount of space offered in Canada's northern national parks is intimidating. With limited backcountry experience, and no idea where to start, the opportunity to fly into a remote camp with hot showers, meals, and experienced guides is a real plus. Exploring the beauty of the valleys, rivers, and mountains of the western Arctic by foot is a shoe-in for the bucket list. And as for the Tasmanian devil, well, it doesn't stand a chance.

START HERE: canadianbucketlist.com/ivvavik

SWALLOW THE SOURTOE COCKTAIL

When you're constantly dealing with different cultures, it's easy to put your foot in it. A friend had told me that a bar in Dawson City serves the most disgusting drink in the world, and I told him he was one stick short of a kebab. Live baby mice in China, boiled spiders in Cambodia, fertilized duck eggs in the Philippines — you generally have to head east to find the tattered fringes of exotic world cuisine; and besides, everyone knows that Canada's beaver tails are not made from real beavers. I had belittled my friend because this "Sourtoe Cocktail" could not possibly be real, with its special ingredient found nowhere on Earth. Actually, it's available everywhere on Earth — it's just very, very odd.

"I'm telling you," he told me, "they drop a severed human toe into a drink."

Really, I just didn't think Canada had it in her.

Dawson City boomed as a major centre of the short-lived Klondike gold rush. Between 1896 and 1898, the population swelled to forty-thousand making it the largest city north of San Francisco. By 1902, the gold had dried up, along with dreams of fame and

fortune. Dawson City quickly turned into a small outpost with sinking wooden storefronts, population 1,300. In 1973, a local eccentric wanted to capitalize on the summer tourist traffic heading to the Top of the World Highway. Captain Dick, as he is known, had recently found a severed toe in an old log cabin. Now, when the temperature plummets to −55°C, hard men are known to do strange things, including, as poet Robert Service famously suggested, setting themselves on fire. Captain Dick dropped the shrivelled toe into a glass of champagne and called it the Sourtoe Cocktail. He started a club, crowning himself the Toe Captain. To join it, all you had to do was order the drink and let the toe touch your lips. Word caught on; a legend was born.

Four decades later, I walk into the Downtown Hotel, chilled to my bones. It's winter, and the icy streets of Dawson are deserted. Captain Al, tonight's Toe Captain, is awaiting new customers at the bar. Behind the counter sits the eighth reincarnation of the original toe, preserved in a jar of salt. Over the years, toes have been stolen, lost, and, in some unfortunate cases, swallowed. My toe for the evening is a sickeningly big appendage donated by an American who lost it in a lawn-mower accident. Every customer gets the same toe. I pay five dollars for the tumbler of Yukon Jack whisky (long since replacing the more expensive champagne) and five dollars to join the club. There's no doubting the authenticity of the digit: yellowed and pickled by the salt, a broken nail crests the top. My stomach lurches, as Captain Al launches into a well-rehearsed ritual:

An Expensive Toe

On August 24, 2013, a young man by the name of Joshua Clark walked into the Downtown Bar and ordered the Sourtoe Cocktail. Suspiciously, he placed five hundred dollars in cash on the table, the exact amount one is fined should something unfortunate happen to the toe. After the usual ceremony, the man slugged back the drink, toe and all. Recorded for YouTube, the night's Toe Captain, Terry Lee, could only stare in disbelief. This was the big toe! Since the incident, the fine has been raised to $2,500. If someone walks into the bar and slaps down the cash on the bar, at least this time the Toe Captain will know what to expect. In the meantime, the new toes are smaller digits, which makes the Sourtoe Cocktail just a little easier to swallow. ➤

"Drink it fast or drink it slow, but either way, your lips must touch this gnarly-looking toe!"

I arch my neck, taste the sweet bourbon, and indulge in this ceremony of cocktail cannibalism. Not too bad. Perhaps a little too much toe jam on the high notes.

Captain Al tells me the club has more than forty thousand members. Anyone of drinking age can join, and since the Downtown Hotel is not responsible for what you put in your drink after it's purchased, the health authorities are powerless to do much about it. Tourists now visit Dawson City specifically to go toe to toe with this challenging libation, much as Captain Dick anticipated. With my name logged in a book, I receive a card confirming membership in the Sourtoe Cocktail Club. I immediately email my friend to apologize for having dismissed his story about a drink with a dismembered human appendage. In my defence, it had been one tough story to swallow, but I should know better than to step on anybody's toes.

START HERE: canadianbucketlist.com/sourtoe

DRIVE THE DEMPSTER HIGHWAY

There are road trips, and then there are adventures. The Dempster Highway, a ghost road built for an oil and gas boom that never came, certainly belongs in the latter category. It begins forty kilometres east of Dawson City and runs north on a narrow gravel strip for some 750 kilometres before eventually reaching Inuvik, in the Northwest Territories. By this stage, most motorists have turned back, happy to have reached the Arctic Circle, just over four hundred kilometres into the journey. Considering that many will already have driven five hundred kilometres from Whitehorse just to get to the starting junction, we'll forgive them.

Decades ago, when the oil trucks abandoned the road, they left a pathway through a land of pristine mountains, valleys, plateaus, and

The World's Smallest Desert

Crossing the Yukon by car, you might want to pop into the aptly named Carcross, located on the South Klondike Highway between Whitehorse and Alaska's Skagway. At just 260 hectares, the nearby Carcross Desert claims to be the world's smallest desert, although geologists prefer to call it the sandy remains of an ancient glacial lake. Either way, the fine grain and terrific views make it ideal for the very desert-like sport of sandboarding. ➤

tundra. Call it the Serengeti of the North, substitute bears for lions, muskox for wildebeest, caribou for antelope, and wolves for hyenas. You'll also find Dall sheep, wild horses, and some two hundred species of birds.

The landscape and wildlife are a perk, but the main priority is getting in and getting out in one piece. This is not the road for just one spare tire. Motorists tell tales of four blowouts in a matter of miles, leaving you stranded as close to the middle of nowhere as you'd ever want to get. Sharp shale shreds tires, and three or even four spares are recommended for the journey. There are no emergency pullouts, and fuel stops can be spaced hundreds of kilometres apart. The name of the highway itself serves as a warning for the unprepared: Corporal Dempster was an RCMP officer who found an RCMP patrol frozen to death after getting lost without a First Nations guide.

Parks Canada has supplied some spartan campgrounds along the way, with no electricity, and pit toilets. They're a welcome refuge, but they won't save you from the relentless bugs in summer. Pitching a tent can be more trouble than it's worth, what with the bears and wolves, so many drivers opt to sleep in their cars. The road unfolds over a landscape that does, however, yield its rewards: epic views of mountains, rivers, and valleys; wildlife crossing the road; fireweed exploding at the end of the short summer. The few motels and gas stations cater to passing traffic, pearls of survival on the endless gravel string. Fresh water is trucked in, and accommodation can fill up quickly. The gravel road

surface is soon replaced by thick mud, with dreaded punctures just a speedometer click away. No wonder so many drivers turn back at the Arctic Circle, their adventure quotient filled to the brim.

If you keep going, the mountain roads become even more challenging, aided by weather that threatens visibility, and sticky mud waiting like flycatchers for cars. In summer, there are ferry services over several rivers, while winter allows cars to drive directly over the ice, including those braving the legendary ALCAN 5000 Rally race. The final stretch to Inuvik consists of a couple of hundred kilometres of tundra before the highway connects to a paved road. After days of dicey gravel, it feels as if the car is floating on air.

So why is such a gruelling road trip on the Northern Bucket List? For starters, it's a lifeline through some of the most desolate and remote scenery you'll find anywhere in the world. A personal challenge of skill, perseverance, and sense of adventure. Canada's North, and all its creatures, await you on a rocky road you'll never forget.

START HERE: canadianbucketlist.com/dawson

YUKON

19

FREEZE YOUR HAIR

I've said it before and I'll say it again: Canada is far weirder than anyone thinks. We've already looked at a cocktail served with a severed human toe, but how about a hair-freezing contest? The Takhini Hot Pools, located twenty-five minutes north of Whitehorse, consists of two connected pools with 35°C waters flowing from deep within the ground. Rich in minerals, reddish in hue, and lacking the sulphur-stink typically found at natural hot springs, these hot waters have been known to locals for generations, with the first wooden pool built in the 1950s by U.S. Army engineers constructing the Alaska Highway.

Filtered daily, the pools are a treat for locals and drivers of the iconic road, but our bucket list shows up in the freeze of February

for the annual Hair Freezing Contest. To enter, simply sculpt your frozen hair, take a photo, post it to Facebook, and let the digital herd decide if you qualify for the largely symbolic cash prize. The trick is to lay your hair on the edge of the pool, wait for it to freeze, and then mould it into something that would give Edward Scissorhands a heart attack. Admittedly, not too many people enter this month-long contest, but it does generate good press, hilarious photos, and a unique experience that will make a fantastic story at dinner parties. If, like me, you don't have enough hair to give the judges something to consider, simply enjoy a refreshing soak.

START HERE: canadianbucketlist.com/takhini

CLIMB THE GOLDEN STAIRS

G-O-L-D — a substance that historically has driven people to the very limits of their mental and physical limits. When gold was discovered in Yukon's Klondike region, it attracted more than one hundred thousand prospectors, insects to a golden flame (and even more likely to be toasted by it). Unlike the San Francisco gold rush a half-century prior, the Klondike was not nearly as accessible. Prospectors had just two options to get to the headwaters of the Yukon River: hike the White Pass route from Skagway, Alaska, or take on the shorter, steeper, and cheaper Chilkoot Trail. Since nobody wants to dawdle when there's gold to be found (it is a gold *rush*, after all), the Chilkoot Trail from Dyea Alaska became known

Before the Gold

The Tlingit were the first to use the Chilkoot Trail as one of five trade routes into the interior. Different clans would manage the trade routes, with the Raven clan in charge of the Chilkoot. The Tlingit traded furs, fish, and clothing with the interior tribes, until European fur traders arrived and became valuable new trading partners. The U.S. Navy later negotiated with the Tlingit so that prospectors could use the trail, with the Tlingit initially profiting from packing services before being unable to keep up with demand. ➤

as the Poor Man's Route to the Klondike. Many of these prospectors had more ambition than sense. After several tragedies, the Northwest Mounted Police insisted that prospectors (also known as "stampeders") only enter Canada if they had at least one ton of gear. Pack mules, aerial tramways, and porters were utilized to schlep this gear from campsite to campsite, crossing coastal rainforest and treacherous high alpine passes to get to the valley below. With some forty cache drops, it was tough going. Leading up to the Chilkoot Pass the trail elevated almost three hundred metres in the final eight hundred metres alone. These were the intimidating Golden Stairs, fifteen hundred steps cut into the ice and snow, leading to riches or misery. The

↑

YUKON

23

mere sight of the pass was enough to send many a defeated stampeder retreating in the opposite direction. In April 1898, unstable weather caused avalanche conditions, and despite warnings from trail guides, prospectors insisted on moving forward. A series of avalanches claimed the lives of more than sixty people in just one day. The following year, the trail became obsolete with the introduction of a railway running along the White Pass. Ironically, 1899 also signalled the end of the Klondike gold rush, as prospectors in Dawson City found no opportunities, and the media hype shifted to the Spanish American War. The boom was over, but the Chilkoot Trail was far from finished.

Each summer, the fifty-three-kilometre trail attracts hikers from around the world, drawn to the spectacular scenery, a rugged challenge, and the enduring draw of history. It constitutes the largest National Historic Site in the country, and in partnership with the United States, is known as the Klondike Gold Rush International Historic Site. Maintained by Parks Canada and the U.S. National Parks Service, just fifty hikers are allowed to enter the trail each day, and due to high demand, reservations are essential. In the ghostly wake of shoddy tent cities are well-maintained campgrounds, interpretative signs, and warden patrols. With slippery, snow-covered rocky terrain, Parks Canada leaves no doubt this is a demanding trail: **"The Chilkoot should only be attempted by persons who are physically fit and experienced in hiking and backpacking."** They bold that, to show they're serious.

YUKON

The Dyea trailhead is accessed via Skagway (a three-hour drive from Whitehorse) with hikers collected at the Bennett, B.C., trailhead by the White Pass and Yukon Route Railway, or by charter plane. It generally takes between three to five days to hike the trail, depending on your pace. Taking on the Golden Stairs and crossing the pass from Sheep Camp to Happy Camp is typically a twelve-hour haul. Once you're over the pass, it gets warmer as you enter the boreal forests, arriving at the gem-coloured Lake Lindeman, and onto Bare Loon Lake and finally Bennett. Today's Chilkoot Trail attracts hikers chasing a different type of gold, although one that I'd argue is no less precious. The gold of the great outdoors, the gold of a physical challenge, and the gold of ticking off an unforgettable experience on the Northern Bucket List.

START HERE: canadianbucketlist.com/chilkoottrail

↑

YUKON

SKATE ON A CRYSTAL LAKE

Hopefully, you've noticed that the items that make up the Great Northern Canada Bucket List rely on things that you can actually do, as opposed to fantasy scenarios that are fun to imagine and all but impossible to experience. This is why you will not find the following:

- Watch two walrus bulls battle under an eclipse.
- Go narwhal watching on an ice flow with Leonardo DiCaprio.
- Scuba dive inside the wreck of the *Erebus*.

When I saw a YouTube clip of a bunch of guys shooting a puck to each other on a mirror-ice lake, surrounded by mountains and with fish swimming beneath them, I had to wonder: can you really do this? Yes, you can. Or, more cleverly, yes, Yu-kon. Granted, the conditions have to be goldilocks, and this does not happen every year. It has to be early winter, when the temperature drops for weeks, the lakes freeze up, but the snow is yet to fall. Alternatively, snow has fallen but heavy wind has scattered the flakes before they can scratch up the smoothness of the lake surface. Every three years or so you'll find these conditions at one of several lakes not far from Whitehorse: Kluane Lake, in the national park; Fish Lake; Kusawa Lake; and the scene of the video that went viral and dropped jaws around the world, Windy Arm on Tagish Lake. It's part of a chain of lakes that form the headwaters of the Yukon River, framed by dramatic mountains that create a tunnel for the wind to barrel through — hence its name.

YUKON

Gather Round, Ye Sourdoughs

You can't just show up in Whitehorse and call yourself a sourdough. The term dates back to the Klondike gold rush, when the name of the hard, fermented bread eaten by locals was bestowed on those who managed to stick around from the freeze of fall to the thaw of spring. Everyone else, well, they were just a bunch of *cheechakos*, a Chinook word for a newcomer. ➤

Local photographer Peter Maher takes his family out every year searching for this type of magic. He'll arrive at the shore and check the ice. Just ten centimetres will do it, since trucks can drive on fifteen centimetres and thrill-seekers might go out on as little as five. Strong winds keep snow off the ice and the surface as smooth as freshly cut glass. Once you're skating, it's a window that reveals schools of grayling or trout swimming beneath you, or bottom-feeders drifting along the sandy depths. Ice bubbles create beautiful art in the ice, smooth pockets of air suspended like frozen thought balloons. You can skate for miles on this pond hockey rink of dreams, although strong winds might blow you farther than you intended. Peter might have someone drive the car ten kilometres down the road to avoid the family having to skate against the wind, which I'm sure his three kids appreciate. He'll whip out his camera and take some remarkable photos.

Once word gets out, locals start showing up with their skates and sticks. There used to be dozens of people, but with Facebook and YouTube spreading the good news, these days there might be hundreds, not to mention people coming in from farther away. Of course, on a lake that stretches over a hundred kilometres, there's plenty of room for everyone, with games of pond hockey featuring twenty or thirty players, all bundled up, carrying Thermos flasks with hot chocolate (or something stronger), gliding on their reflections in a real-life fantasy.

"This is one of the things that makes being a Canadian so special," says Peter. And while you may not be able to show up and do this every winter, it's special enough, distinctly Canadian enough, and real enough to make it onto the Northern Bucket List.

START HERE: canadianbucketlist.com/windyarm

CHEER AT THE ARCTIC GAMES

Every two years, participants from Northern Canada, Greenland, Northern Scandinavia, Alaska, Iceland, and the Russian province of Yupa gather for a chillier alternative to the Winter Olympics. Founded in 1970, the Arctic Games was designed to "furnish the opportunity through sport, the social and cultural meeting of Northern peoples regardless of language, race, or creed."

Regional and territorial trials whittle down the field until only the best athletes compete in different sports across three categories: major sports (such as hockey, volleyball, indoor soccer, cross-country skiing), traditional sports (including Inuit and Dene events, dog-mushing, snowshoeing), and emerging sports (such as

snowboarding and table tennis). A new location hosts the March event biennially, proudly drawing upwards of 1,500 athletes from more than one hundred towns, villages, hamlets, and communities across the Arctic.

The Inuit sports include the thrilling one-foot and two-foot high kick, the knuckle hop, sledge jump, and one-hand reach, all involving impressive strength, agility, and skill. I tried a one-foot kick once, attempting to tap the high hanging target and land on the same foot. My testicles have never forgiven me. Dene sports include the finger pull, pole push, and the snow snake, a spear-tossing game inspired by caribou hunting techniques.

It's a festive atmosphere throughout, with medallists awarded a distinctive Arctic Games ulu-shaped medal, and a colourful closing ceremony celebrating the very best of life in the North. You might not find yourself in Nuuk, Greenland, or Fairbanks, Alaska, but when the games once again visit Whitehorse, Yellowknife, or other Canadian host towns, come on up to support the Olympics of the North.

PAN FOR GOLD

The Klondike gold rush of 1898 was a boom that could be heard around the world. Although it was short-lived, you can still hear the faint whispers of its allure — the seductive promise of instant wealth — with a visit to Dawson City and a half-hour drive to Gold Bottom. Once a town of five thousand people, Gold Bottom has just five residents these days, all still involved in active gold mining. During the summer months (−40°C weather doesn't draw too many visitors), you can sign up for a panning tour and sift through real pay dirt, with the bonus of being able to keep whatever you find.

As you slip on your rubber boots and load your thirty-six-centimetre metal pan with rocks and gravel, spare a thought for the hardened prospectors who came before you. When word finally got out about streams of gold discovered up north, some one hundred thousand people flocked to the Yukon in search of glory. Dawson City, a ramshackle outpost, became the largest Canadian city west of Winnipeg. The boom was such that a single room in Dawson might rent for one hundred dollars a month, when a four-bedroom apartment in New York City could be had for only $120. Only forty thousand people accomplished the four-hundred–kilometre journey through the rugged winter landscape. To stake a claim on the Klondike and surrounding rivers, they had to bring everything with them and face months of dirty, back-breaking work. Unfortunately, by the time the majority of prospectors arrived, most of the claims had been staked, the gold extracted, poems written, and fortunes made. It didn't take long for booming Dawson to sink back into the ghost towns of history, its proud saloons literally sinking into the permafrost.

Parks Canada and the government came to the rescue in the 1960s, restoring the town as a National Historic Site, preserved for the thousands of tourists who visit each year. People come from around the world for the history, the quirks (see Sourtoe Cocktail, page 13), the scenery, the drives, and the boom-time legends. Such as Chris Johansen, a miner on Hunker Creek, who offered one Cecile Marion her weight in gold if she would be his wife — an offer that cost him $25,000 when the sixty-one-kilo beauty agreed.

It was the same Hunker Creek where David Millar is now bent over and facing upriver, explaining how to pan the pay dirt. His family has been operating the Gold Bottom mining camp for more than three decades, expanding it with rustic log cabins and daily tours, rain or shine. Calf-deep in the muddy brown water, he fills the pan with water, shaking it gently at first while picking out the big rocks. Dipping the pan at a forty-five-degree angle, he adds more water, the pan is spun and shaken, the gravel slowly rinsed and discarded. Gold is nineteen times heavier than water, so you'll know you've got something when you spot tiny flakes resting at the bottom of the pan. It's a slow process for first-timers, and you might walk away with anywhere between one and ten flakes.

Tips for Panning for Gold

1. Fill your pan halfway to three-quarters of the way to the top with silt. Pick out the bigger rocks, looking for nuggets as you do so.

2. Find a spot where the river flows strongly enough to carry away the silt from your pan. Sit on a log or rock unless you're particularly bendy.

3. Dip your pan in the water, using your fingers to sort the dirt and moss. Heavy gold will sink to the bottom of your submerged pan.

4. Shake the pan while it's submerged, breaking up the silt even more, allowing any gold to sink and silt to rise to the top.

5. Tilt the pan downwards, shaking the pan some more.

6. Submerge the pan again, shaking it up and down and left to right, allowing the river to wash away the lighter material. Tilt occasionally, rinse, and repeat. Keep checking to see if any gold has sunk to the bottom.

7. Use tweezers or a wet finger to extract your treasure.

8. Cash it in, and blow it all at the local saloon. ➤

In the meantime, expect to learn about the entire process, hear about the gold rush, and even see mammoth bones, teeth, and tusks that have been discovered by miners digging into the permafrost. There's an eight-centimetre nugget on display in the mine's Gold Lodge, and enough value in the area to keep several mines in profitable operation. As you walk away with a vital keepsake, your hard-won treasures certainly won't be worth much in value, but panning at Gold Bottom, unlike prospecting in the nineteenth century, is all about the experience.

START HERE: canadianbucketlist.com/goldpan

YUKON ↑

FLY OVER KLUANE NATIONAL PARK

About two hours' drive from Whitehorse along the famed Alaska Highway lies the sleepy little town of Haines Junction. There's not a heck of a lot going on, besides hikers and climbers hanging out at the bakery and an impressive new cultural museum celebrating the life and times of the region's Champagne and Aishihik people. The town receives a fair amount of passing traffic made up of RVs, motorbikes, and cars making their way north, enjoying hour after hour of snow-capped mountains, valleys, and glaciers, as well as the occasional moose or elk. From the road, you simply have no idea what lies beyond those first peaks — the striking and magnificent wilderness encompassed by the twenty-two-thousand-square-kilometre Kluane National Park and Reserve. And although you can stop for a hike around crystal-clear Kathleen Lake, even climbing a nearby peak, there are limits to where your legs can take you.

Which is why I'm sitting in a six-seat Cessna 205 operated by Sifton Air, embarking on a one-hour flightseeing tour. Call me a Robin with a bird's-eye view of the world's largest non-polar ice caps, the continent's tallest mountains, and an alien world of rock and ice.

The altimeter wobbles at six thousand metres when we first see the Kaskawulsh Glacier, a massive river of moving ice that S-curves through a chain of mountains, carving out a valley with all the patience in the universe. Eighty-two percent of Kluane's surface area consists of mountain and ice. The scale of this natural beauty even has our pilot reaching for his camera, a man who flies this route daily during the summer tourist season. In the context of endless ice, giant rockfalls, and serrated granite peaks, our plane feels as small as a gnat, and my adjectives thin as toothpicks. We fly up the glacier, hoping for a glimpse of Mount Logan to the east. Almost six kilometres tall, the largest mountain in Canada also boasts the largest base circumference of any mountain on earth, including the giants found in the Himalayas. The tallest peak on the continent, Denali, takes up residence farther north, in Alaska, and together with other plus five-thousand-metre peaks found in the area, it's clear why climbers have been coming here for decades.

Today, fortunately, is not one for ropes and harnesses, to cling to life by my fingertips. Although the Cessna bounces around in the thermals, rattling and roller-coastering, I've learned that such turbulence presents as much of a problem for planes as small bumps in the road do for cars. Even though it's a crisp summer day, Mount Logan is hidden in the clouds, so we bank left and make our way towards Kluane's most impressive wall of ice, the seventy-kilometre-long, five-kilometre-wide Lowell Glacier. When moist Pacific air collides with these Arctic air masses, it results in huge amounts of snow, compacted over time into glaciers. Lowell's surges and ice

Canada's Highest Mountain

Located within Kluane National Park is Canada's Mount Logan, towering at 5,959 metres. Even if it does take second place to Alaska's Denali, North America's highest mountain, Logan is still higher than any mountain in Africa, Europe, or Oceania. It has the largest base circumference of any non-volcanic mountain on Earth. ➤

dams have resulted in devastating floods, with local legends recalling whole villages being washed away by tsunamis of mountain water.

Down below I see deep crevices, cut like scars into the ice, and pools of ice-blue water, some of the purest drinking water on Earth. We trace the glacier, watching it break apart into braided streams and muddy silt, and continue the journey over stunted forests of aspen, spruce, and poplar. I'm keeping my eyes peeled for bear and moose, and spot a half-dozen white Dall sheep, the park's most abundant mammal, impossibly perched high atop a mountain.

The hour-long flight is almost complete, and I've seen just a fraction of this vast open space, the flora and fauna hidden from above like secrets. Most of Kluane is accessible only by air, hence the flightseeing options available in Haines Junction. Hop on board a plane or helicopter and witness the blue ice and black rock brush strokes on a truly spectacular Canadian canvas.

START HERE: canadianbucketlist.com/kluane

STRETCH YOUR LEGS (AND STOMACH)

About an hour and fifteen minutes' drive from Whitehorse, on the way to Dawson City, is a pit stop famous for pee breaks, stretching one's legs, and cinnamon buns the size of dinner plates. Baked on site, there's nothing particularly spectacular about these buns, other than the fact that you could probably feed a small village in Liberia with just one. Braeburn also happens to be a checkpoint on the Yukon Quest, so perhaps the size of the buns is meant to encourage mushers with an overload of gooey, melt-in-the-mouth calories. For those with a more savoury bent, Braeburn Lodge also serves oversize hamburgers as large as dinner plates.

↑

YUKON

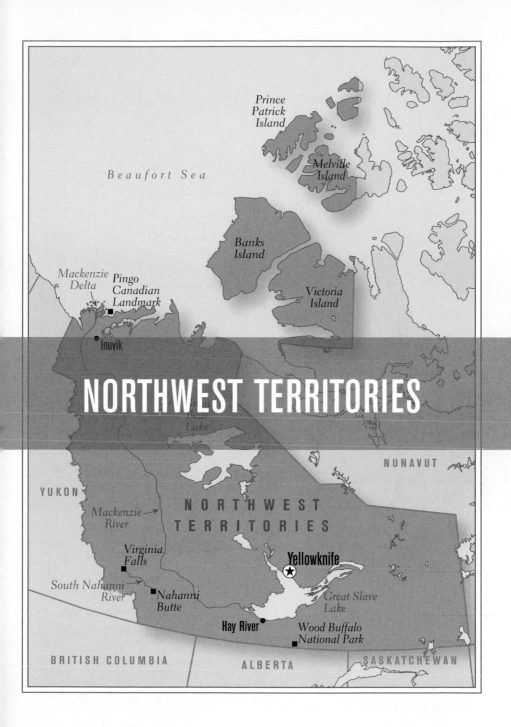

NORTHWEST TERRITORIES

Prince
Patrick
Island

Beaufort Sea

Melville
Island

Banks
Island

Mackenzie
Delta

Pingo
Canadian
Landmark

Victoria
Island

Inuvik

Bear
Lake

NUNAVUT

YUKON

Mackenzie
River

NORTHWEST
TERRITORIES

Virginia
Falls

Yellowknife

South Nahanni
River

Nahanni
Butte

Great Slave
Lake

Hay River

Wood Buffalo
National Park

BRITISH COLUMBIA

ALBERTA

SASKATCHEWAN

SEE THE NORTHERN LIGHTS

It's my tenth failed attempt to see the northern lights, and here's my conclusion: When you live in cold, sparsely populated northern climes, surrounded by unimaginable amounts of space, your mind begins to untangle. Brain unwinding, it fires relaxing neurons into the backs of your eyeballs, resulting in beautiful hallucinations that can best be described as "lights dancing across the sky." When a traveller arrives from out of town with hopes of experiencing such a phenomenon, here's what he'll hear:

1. You should have been here last week, they were incredible!
2. You should be here next week, they'll be incredible!

Being here right now, on the other hand, results in clear skies with no dancing lights, or foggy skies with no dancing lights, or rainy nights with twelve Japanese tourists looking glumly toward the sky. This was my experience when I spent two weeks in Alaska. Ditto for a week in the Yukon. Likewise a week in northern Saskatchewan, and now, during a week in the best place to view the alleged natural light show, right below the aurora belt in Yellowknife.

Adding to my misery is the fact that my dad has flown up from Vancouver to join me, as viewing the aurora borealis has been the number one item on his bucket list ever since he saw an awful eighties movie called *St. Elmo's Fire*, which does not actually feature the aurora borealis but does contain the light going out of Ally Sheedy's acting career. Bucket lists are personal, and I'm not one to question, but we still pass on Grant Beck's offer to visit his comfortable Aurora Watching cabin on a cold, rainy night when Yellowknife is consumed by a permanent cloud. Grant, a champion dog musher who also runs mushing tours, is being wonderfully optimistic. "Sometimes the clouds break, and we get a beautiful show!" he tells us. You can almost hear those nerves crackling behind his retinas.

We would spend the night with a dozen Japanese tourists, who visit Yellowknife in the belief that procreating beneath the northern lights ushers in extremely good luck for any resulting babies. Of course, they're not seeing the lights if they're actually procreating, at least not in front of us.

Northerners tell us that the fabled northern lights are the result of electrical storms caused by solar flares smashing into Earth's magnetic field. Yellowknife sits directly under the aurora oval, where these lights can be seen at their most brilliant, attracting tourists from around the world in the hope that they, too, will share in this mass hallucination. Every local I meet is eager to share a story of the sky exploding in luminous shades of green, red, and blue, "like, just last week, on the day before you arrived."

The rain continues to fall, but it doesn't dampen the spirits of Carlos Gonzalez at Yellowknife Outdoor Adventures. After all, we'd just spent the day fishing on Great Slave, and Carlos has seen the skies part like the Red Sea before. Just not tonight. The weather forecast is looking fantastic, however, for the day after we leave.

Thanks to Buffalo Air, we are now in Hay River. It's cloudy, of course, which makes for poor (that is, impossible) aurora viewing. Before retiring for the night at the town's Ptarmigan Inn, we ask the friendly receptionist, half-heartedly, to call us if he notices, oh, a natural fireworks display in the sky. Imagine, then, our reactions when the hotel phone wakes us shortly after midnight with exciting news! The sky, would you believe, is absolutely clear — but there are no lights in it. Seriously, guy?

At two a.m., the phone rings again. Something about lights in the sky. My dad is at the door before I open my eyes, and I meet him in the parking lot, looking somewhat perplexed, repeatedly asking: "Where, where, where?" I direct his attention to a faint glow above us, and the fact that we're standing under a rather bright street light. We walk a couple of blocks to the river, where there's less light pollution,

and sure enough, a huge green band is glowing in the sky. To our right, spectacular bolts of lightning are firing on the horizon. To our left, a bright, half-crescent yellow moon bobs in the purple sky. My dad puts his arm around me, a huge smile on his face. "Will you look at that!" he says in amazement. Yep, I can see it clearly.

We've officially spent too much time in the North, and now we're starting to hallucinate too.

START HERE: canadianbucketlist.com/aurora

FLY WITH BUFFALO AIR

You don't need a hit international TV show to see that Yellowknife's Buffalo Airways is the world's coolest airline. With a fleet of more than fifty planes, including a dozen DC-3s and DC-4s, no other airline can transport you back to the Golden Age of Flying the way these folks do. It's why guys like Andrew Bromage sit in Buffalo's humble departure lounge, having flown all the way from Liverpool to fly Buffalo Air on his birthday. Why Germans, Americans, and Australians arrive almost daily to walk among planes that have as much character as the people who operate them. All decked in a distinctive "Northern Light" green, with the fragrance of grease and sound family values.

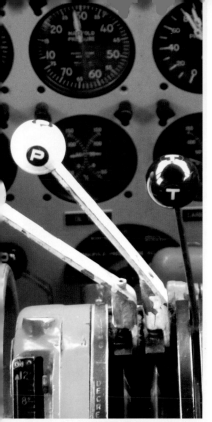

Your Pilot May Look Familiar

From *The Deadliest Catch* to *Ice Road Truckers* to *Flying Wild Alaska*, TV audiences love the extreme lifestyles and personalities of men and women of the North. With its retro colours, larger-than-life characters and dangerous working environment, it was just a matter of time before Buffalo Air flew high in the world of television. Originally produced for the History Channel by Vancouver-based Omni Film (the same company that produced my own series *Word Travels*, using many of the same crew), *Ice Pilots* has been seen on networks including National Geographic around the world, making stars of its very authentic owners, managers, pilots, and maintenance crew. There's even an Ice Pilots roller coaster in Denmark's Legoland Park. When these old birds are flying, though, you can rest assured the folks at Buffalo Air are more concerned with service and safety than with television ratings. ➤

Operating largely as a supply lifeline to remote northern communities, Buffalo's "ice pilots" and planes are renowned for handling conditions that would freeze the cockpit off a commercial jet. Fortunately, they also fly a scheduled passenger service across Great Slave Lake to Hay River, a short flight I was eager to board. Once the stalwart of Second World War–era air forces and airlines, Buffalo's tail-wheel DC-3s look like props from an Indiana Jones movie. Tilting upward, the lime-coloured interior features large windows and an open cockpit. With Chief Pilot Justin Simle at the helm, we're in exceptionally safe hands. Buffalo operates the world's largest fleet of DC-3s, which is why it was well known to plane enthusiasts long before it became the focus of the hit reality show *Ice Pilots*.

"It's the planes that are the stars of the show," says Justin, although credit must be given to the airline's distinctly human element, starting with founder "Buffalo Joe" McBryan. He's taken only two days off in forty-two years, and one of them was for his honeymoon. The family are all involved: youngest son Mikey is the general manager,

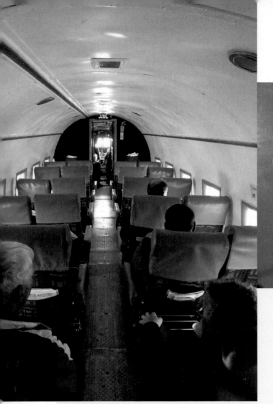

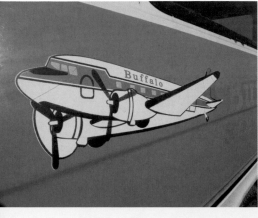

Rod is the director of maintenance, and daughter Kathy runs operations in Hay River. Visitors are invited to visit the hangar and take a look around, where they'll be surprised to learn the characters on TV are very much the characters in real life. Crusty Chuck is literally greasing the wheels, while Sophie the mutt wanders about, a dog that has logged more flight time than many commercial pilots.

Justin shows me around the interior of a powerful Lockheed Electra, as well as Buffalo's water bombers (sorry, Mordecai Richler's ghost, but it's impossible for a bomber to suck up a swimmer in a lake). I'm itching to get in the air, and it's time for the four-thirty departure to Hay River. While Buffalo operates according to the same regulations as any commercial airline in Canada, the age of its planes and the attitudes of its crew are distinctly different. "We've got little interest in modern aviation. That's like sitting in a doctor's office," explains Mikey. "Most pilots want to be in a suit walking through a terminal. Our guys love adventure."

How refreshing to see pilots in jeans, and the formalities taken care of with the distinct understanding that, yes, I know how to operate a seat belt, and no, handstands in the aisles during turbulence is not a wise idea. The props roar to life, and in a surprisingly short take-off the DC-3 tilts forward and gently floats into the big northern sky.

It's a smooth ride at 1,500 metres above the lake, and with the pilot's permission, passengers can poke their heads into the cockpit, perhaps even take the jump seat and ask some questions. The forty-five-minute flight to the small transport hub of Hay River is fun, fascinating, and, I suppose, what flying used to be like.

Fortunately, Buffalo's influence now extends to ensuring there's something to do in Hay River when you get there. Together with her husband, Fraser, and stepson Spencer, Kathy McBryan has launched Hay River's first tour operator, 2 Seasons Adventures. Guests can spend the night in a yurt or cabin on the sandy beaches of Great Slave, hop aboard an ATV, go fishing, or ski, snowmobile, and ice-fish in the winter; take a jet boat to Louise Falls, party on a barge, spend the night watching the northern lights, or enjoy a barbecue on the boat as they float up the Mackenzie River. "There's so much to do here," says hunky Spencer as he cuts a Polaris ATV into the forest. All you need are locals with the right toys, toys that 2 Seasons has in abundance.

Back in Yellowknife, the distinctly green DC-3 lands on the runway. Nobody is quite sure what possessed Joe to adopt the colour, and four decades of aviation life in the northern extremes have blurred fact and myth, even for the founder. Maybe it's because he was born on St. Patrick's Day, or perhaps it was to remember the first green planes he ever flew. One thing's for sure: it makes for memorable merchandise in the gift shop. "People would come and demand souvenirs, and it's just grown from there," explains Peter, as we stand in the merchandise store. Everyone's wearing something that says "Buffalo," and by the end of my visit it's hard to distinguish who's a passenger, a visitor, a pilot, or a member of the crew.

For making flying fun again — on the ground, in the air and on TV too — Buffalo Air buzzes the Great Northern Canada Bucket List.

START HERE: canadianbucketlist.com/buffaloair

EXPLORE CANADA'S LARGEST NATIONAL PARK

Wood Buffalo National Park, split between Alberta and the Northwest Territories, has an area of 44,807 square kilometres. In Europe, they might call that a country, a country the size of Denmark, and bigger than Switzerland. Wood Buffalo, I might add, has no people living in it.

Established in 1922 as northern Canada's first national park, and the country's largest, Wood Buffalo is a massive stretch of land that protects, among other creatures, the last free-roaming wood bison herds in the world. Bison were once prolific, roaming in boreal forests from Saskatchewan to British Columbia and all the way north to the Yukon, Alaska, and the Northwest Territories, but unchecked

Space? We've Got It

Two new national parks were announced in August 2015. Mealy Mountains, located in Labrador, offi-cially became Canada's forty-sixth national park, and it's the size of Jamaica! In co-operation with the Lutsel K'e Dene First Nation, the Northwest Territories government also set aside an enormous area for the Thaidene Nene National Park Reserve. Canada's ten largest national parks, protected from oil, gas, or human development, are all found in the North.

1. Wood Buffalo, NT/AB (44,807 km^2)
2. Quttinirpaaq, NU (37,775 km^2)
3. Nahanni, NT (30,000 km^2)
4. Sirmilik, NU (22,200 km^2)
5. Kluane, YK (22,013 km^2)
6. Ukkusiksalik, NU (20,885 km^2)
7. Auyuittuq, NU (19,089 km^2)
8. Tuktut Nogait, NT (16,340 km^2)
9. Thaidene Nene National Park Reserve, NT (14,000 km^2)
10. Aulavik, NT (12,200 km^2) ➤

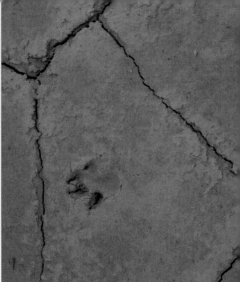

hunting and severe winters took them to the very brink of extinction. At the end of the nineteenth century there were fewer than 250 animals left. Thanks to the efforts of conservationists and Parks Canada, their numbers have rebounded to around ten thousand, with half of those living in Wood Buffalo National Park.

Joining them in this vast expanse of wilderness are bears, moose, wolverines, beavers, otters, and the world's largest wolves. Fortuitously, the park also provides protection for a migratory flock of whooping cranes, another species flying back from the brink. In 1941, there were just twenty-one left in existence. Today, Wood Buffalo is home to some three hundred whooping cranes, nesting in a remote corner of the park. Birdwatchers rejoice!

I drive the long road in from Hay River, carving through dense forests of aspen, poplar, spruce, and Jack pine, hoping to see some animals. Canadian wildlife can be painfully shy at the best of times, never mind in the country's biggest national park. Still, I catch a glimpse of a black bear, and a sassy red fox welcomes me to Fort Smith, Wood Buffalo's nearest town.

Here, I meet Parks Canada's Richard Zaidan, who takes me on an introductory visit into this vast, protected wilderness. Our first stop is the Salt River Day Area, the trailhead for five popular hikes, where we stroll the 750-metre Kartsland Loop. Gypsum and limestone have created an extensive cave system beneath our feet, of special benefit to our slithery friend, the red garter snake. Similar to the dens in Narcisse (Manitoba), hundreds of snakes hibernate in these sinkholes and cracks for the winter. Next we drive to Salt Plains and Grosbeak Lake, finding mineral-rich mud with a dusting of white salt, the landscape looking distinctly Martian. Glaciers deposited thousands of rocks in the copper-red mud, mud that is ideal for capturing our footprints along with those of other recent visitors — bison, wolf, and human. Then we visit the public campsites at Pine Lake, where algae have turned the water a rich shade of aquamarine. Easy to see why it's so popular in the summer months, but it's the drive home that introduces us to the park's star attraction.

Three large bulls stand on the side of the dirt road, each hulking rump carrying an enormous head. If the bugs are bad enough to necessitate us donning bug nets at times, these beasts have no chance. Clouds of blackflies surround them, forcing one to rub itself in the dust for relief. Parked just metres away, their bulk is intimidating, even from the relatively safe confines of the pickup truck. It's quite the moment, staring down some of the biggest wild bison in the world, here in Canada's biggest national park. Wood Buffalo has a space on the bucket list, and it's a very large space indeed.

START HERE: canadianbucketlist.com/woodbuffalo

DOWN FISH AND CHIPS AT BULLOCKS

After years in the ho-hum drum, Canada's food scene has blossomed. We've got some of the finest restaurants on the continent, operated by rock star chefs of wildly diverse backgrounds. When a restaurant becomes synonymous with a provincial capital, it demands investigation — especially when reports range from "essential" to "avoid at all costs." Such is the case with Bullocks Bistro, a ramshackle fish shack in Old Town Yellowknife. With a reputation for serving the most expensive fish 'n' chips in Canada, and an open kitchen run by a legendary local character, it demanded a culinary investigation.

Established by husband and wife Sam and Renata Bullock in 1989, the bistro has grown from a simple wooden fish shack into a larger wooden fish shack, covered in bumper stickers, notices, and the satisfied scrawling left by decades of happy customers. The potato chipper is against the wall, the cold beers are in the fridge, and the place has the feel of a warm, frat-house family kitchen. The menu consists of northern seafood delights — pickerel, whitefish, lake trout, Arctic char — grilled, pan-fried, or deep-fried. For the carnivore, there's also grilled caribou, muskox, and bison steaks. No chicken, no beef, only food you can find in the North, all served with a fresh salad and homemade fries. Sam sources and personally fillets all the fresh fish, most caught in Great Slave Lake, just a block away. Renata is the wisecracking chef on the other end of the long wooden counter, unhurriedly carving huge hunks of meat, prepping, grilling, frying and chatting, with the customers. "The North is hot and cold, like menopause," she jokes, and apparently her mood can swing that way too. Tonight she's hot, cackling away with a motherly warmth while Jewel and Junior (and occasionally a customer at the counter) serve the dishes to the busy tables, packed with Japanese tourists and adoring locals.

"Nothing in Yellowknife comes close to this sort of quality," enthuses a mining consultant. Quality *and* quantity, for the portions are noticeably large. Slabs of meat cover the dinner plates, while fish fillets are as large as a basketball player's hands. A patron next to me receives her dish, and Renata adds another large piece of fish because her huge portion didn't look huge enough.

I order Arctic char sashimi to start, a lovely salmon-like fish best enjoyed up north. Next up is the pan-fried pickerel. Renata uses a large chunk of butter, so much that the fish isn't so much fried as poached. It is cooked to perfection, prepared with a sweet-spicy garlic herb mix that hits all the right notes. The salad is fresh and simple, with the choice of a house-made vinaigrette or a rich, creamy feta cheese dressing. Crispy fries taste like real potatoes.

The secret, according to Renata, is the cold waters of Great Slave. The colder the water, the sweeter and fresher the fish. With a dozen meals on the go, she chats away, somehow finding time to show some Japanese tourists where the bathroom light is. The meat is medium rare, the fish melts in your mouth. With a cold Pilsner from the fridge, I read the bumper stickers:

Do you know why divorce is expensive? Because it's worth it!

Mall Wart: Your Choice for Cheap Plastic Crap.

Prices Subject to Customer Attitude.

I'd been forewarned about the cost of visiting Bullocks. A meal for two typically costs around $125. Renata shrugs it off. This is Yellowknife, the nearest big city is 1,700 kilometres away. The fish is as fresh as it gets (the Arctic char is flown in daily), and hey, she reminds me, "If you want an experience, it's gonna cost you!"

An experience is right. Some people might balk at the prices, others at the attitude. But having eaten in hundreds of restaurants around the country, I can say with confidence that few meals are as synonymous with their city, or as memorable, as Bullocks Bistro.

START HERE: canadianbucketlist.com/bullocks

EAT THE MUKTUK

I'll be the first to admit that Inuit-inspired dishes are unlikely to find their way to your local mall's food court. No spicy curries, noodles, or hot cheese. While the North certainly offers delightful dishes prepared with unusual local ingredients (spruce tip jelly! morels!) the Inuvialuit and Gwi'chin feast on delicacies that one might call an acquired taste (and they'll be the first to admit that, too). When poor weather cancelled my day's excursion to see the pingos outside the small hamlet of Tuktoyaktuk, the owners of Inuvik's Up North Tours, Kyle Kisoun-Taylor and his formidable uncle, Jerry Kisoun, warmly invited me to their kitchen to sample some local flavours. Although

Life in a Northern Town

Inuvik, the last stop on the Dempster Highway, was built in the 1960s as a regional centre for the western Arctic. In summer, it sees a steady traffic of RVs and tour bikes, and it
is home to the region's only hospital. An excellent visitor centre explores the cultural and
natural history of the western Arctic.

A curious note: the local liquor store has the best prices for Scotch I've seen anywhere
in the country. Dining is limited, but don't miss the fish tacos and reindeer chilli at Alestines,
served out of an old yellow school bus. Supplies can be procured at the NorthMart supermarket. Given the distances they have to travel, some things are understandably expensive,
and others surprisingly reasonable. While the town once boasted half a dozen pubs, at the
time of writing there is only the Legion, Shivers, and the notorious Trappers, which has the
ambiance of a Wild West Saloon. With a major new road being constructed to Tuktoyaktuk,
there are hopes that tourism will increase in the area, serviced by a small but impressive
airport and a welcoming community of characters. ➤

dining options are limited in the town, I'd already been impressed with the muskox and brie burger I'd devoured at the Mackenzie Hotel, and the fresh and flavourful whitefish tacos served out of a yellow school bus at Alestines. Tonight's menu, however, would be a different kettle of dehydrated fish altogether.

Dried meats and fish form a large part of the northern diet, with Kyle slicing thin strips of both on a cardboard cutting board and placing them in an electric dehydrator. Let's start with whale meat. It looks not unlike jerky, but tastes like the meat of a cow fed a strict diet of sardines. The fishy-meaty taste doesn't exactly roll off the taste buds. Next to the whale is a plate with similar-looking dried beaver, which tastes exactly how you'd imagine a large aquatic rodent to taste, sprinkled with the special flavour of guilt that accompanies any national animal on the menu. The dried reindeer is more recognizable tasting like venison — lean and gamey. More appealing is the boiled tundra swan, which is deliciously ducky, while dried strips of whitefish are suitably complemented by large wads of butter. Dried seal meat also looks like jerky but with a fatty, pungent fishiness to it as well. I guess mammals truly are what they eat. The star of the show, besides Jerry's stories, is traditional *muktuk*, that is, raw baby beluga whale. Cut into small pieces, it is very rich in Vitamin C (in case you were wondering why indigenous northern people don't get scurvy) and looks very much like … well, the skin of a raw baby beluga. Since my toddler has subjected me to hour upon hour of Raffi's classic hit "Baby Beluga," the song spins its notes in my head as I reach for a firm, spongy square. Jerry suggests less chewing and more swallowing, especially with the cartilage texture. "Swim so fine and you swim so free …" Raffi is killing me. I plop the piece in my mouth and instantly realize that muktuk is a dish best left to those who can appreciate it, like family friends who pop over for a visit and take great delight with the smorgasbord on offer. Jerry further explains that muktuk must be served right or else one risks contracting botulism. This particular whale was hunted last season, and only sees light outside the freezer on special occasions. It's a tough whale to swallow. With enough time, one can acquire a taste for whale, although, as comedian Jackie Mason once remarked, one never has to acquire a taste for french fries.

My favourite dish of the evening is frozen Arctic char, served raw to melt in my mouth like ice-cream sashimi. Somewhere between salmon and trout, char is the Northern cuisine's most sought-after fish. The evening is also memorable for the traditional clothing. At one point I try on a seal jacket, polar bear mitts, beaver hat, and wolf boots. Wool and Goretex don't stand a chance. It is easy to understand why animals play such a vital role in Arctic Aboriginal culture.

The weather never does ease up for my visit to Tuktoyaktuk, which, along with Herschel Island, belongs on my Northern Bucket List. It does, however, allow time for a boat ride up the extraordinary Mackenzie Delta, listening to Jerry's stories of growing up in the region, taking his team of dogs out in the winter to trap, hunt, and visit family in the delta. With a Gwi'chin mom and Inuvialuit dad, Jerry knows both worlds, pointing out places from his childhood in the labyrinth of waterways. I see more than a dozen beaver, slapping their tails at our approach. Graceful tundra swans rest on the grassy banks. The mosquitoes are pretty fierce, but this is life in an Arctic summer. Jerry gets a sparkle in his eye recalling the dog teams that gave him so much freedom as a child, and as an adult, too. A peachy sun radiates a special glow at midnight, a purity in the light that has to be experienced at least once in one's life. As for snacks on board: delicious homemade cookies, courtesy of Jerry's wife. Sweet, buttery, and agreeably muktuk-free.

START HERE: canadianbucketlist.com/inuvik

Our Lady of Victory
Roman Catholic Church
Sunday Mass - 11:00 am   Weekday Mass - 5:15 pm
Parish Priest & Parish Office - 180 MacKenzie Rd.   Ph. (867) 777-2236
The church was blessed by Bishop Paul Piché on August 5, 1960

VISIT AN IGLOO CHURCH

The first time I visited Europe, I suffered from church fatigue. It happens to the best of tourists, visiting one soaring cathedral after another. In Southeast Asia, they call it temple fatigue, and they also use the phrase "Same Same but Different" to describe the repetition of menus, or souvenirs, or temples. I mention this because it is exceedingly rare to encounter a church that doesn't look like any other church on Earth. Such is the case with Our Lady of Victory in Inuvik, more popularly known as the Igloo Church.

Nunavut Has One, Too

In Iqaluit, it was Queen Elizabeth II who broke ground with a silver spade on a similar igloo-shaped Anglican church in 1972. Built by Inuit carpenters, St. Jude's Cathedral featured a rotund base beneath a spire and cross. In 2005, the church was destroyed by arson, although many of the interior artifacts were fortunately salvaged from the fire. After years of fundraising, the igloo church was rebuilt and opened in 2012 at a cost of eight million dollars. The Anglican Diocese of the Arctic is the largest in the world, covering an area of four million square kilometres. ➤

No, it is not made of ice.

In 1958, Inuvik was emerging atop the permafrost as the new capital of the western Arctic. The government had decided to base itself here due to its position, on a stretch of flat land and sheltered from the wind. Nearby Aklavik, which actually had a local population, was considered too vulnerable to flooding in the Mackenzie Delta. The Catholic Church sent a priest from Quebec named Brother Maurice Larocque, who was inspired to build a church that reflected the arctic environment, a building that would be simple yet meaningful. A skilled carpenter, he designed the Igloo Church without a blueprint, just a guide of a few lines on a piece of plywood. Timber was boated almost two thousand kilometres down the Mackenzie River from Fort Smith, along with gravel to create an insulation bed. It took two years to build the striking exterior, complemented with stained-glass windows, embossing, and interior religious artwork by a young artist named Mona Thrasher. Sharing the same name as the iconic Notre Dame cathedral in Paris, Our Lady of Victory officially opened in 1960, and today is the most photographed attraction in town. Each Christmas, the church holds a popular concert in English, Gwich'in, and Inuvialuktun, as well as a performance from a local Filipino choir, reflecting the shifting demographics of the region. Tagalog carols in an Arctic igloo church? Now that's different.

START HERE: canadianbucketlist.com/igloochurch

RAFT THE NAHANNI

ell's Gate, Deadmen Valley, Funeral Range, Headless Creek: rafting the South Nahanni River sounds lawless, wild and untamed. It's certainly attracted its fair share of adventurers, from crusty prospectors and Pierre Trudeau to today's modern bucket-lister. Awaiting all is five hundred kilometres of untouched Northwest Territories, comprising vast mountain chains, 1,400-metre-high canyons, evergreen forests and twisting waterways. It's not easy to get there: first you have to get to Yellowknife, then fly or drive to Fort Simpson, and from there charter a float plane over the Nahanni mountain range to the base of Virginia Falls. It's quite the starting line: a spectacular ninety-six-metre-high waterfall, almost twice the height of Niagara Falls. Early explorers wrote how they could hear

its thunder from more than thirty kilometres away. Bucket-listers — as opposed to hard-core rafters, who might start much farther up the river — typically employ the services of professional raft operators who take care of the logistics, portages, cooking, and rafting. All you have to do is go along for the ride, and although you'll pass rapids (including one eight-kilometre stretch and a particular churning soup called the Figure Eight, or Hell's Gate), professional help means the excursion is manageable for virgin rafters.

Each morning, the week-long trip presents a scenic jewel, as you float with the current down a series of four spectacular canyons. Within the stunted tundra, there is also hope of spotting some northern wildlife: bears, Dall sheep, caribou, wolves. Passing through a hairpin

Hikeable, If Not Climbable

Beyond the rafting adventures, Nahanni National Park Reserve gives one an opportunity to hike to an imposing semicircle of peaks christened by a group of American rock climbers as the "Cirque of the Unclimbables." Granite walls 2,740 metres high dramatically face each other, forming an imposing amphitheatre. Kicking off from Glacier Lake, day-trippers to the "Unclimbables" can get dramatic views by hiking up to a viewpoint. You will also encounter Rabbitkettle Lake, the largest tufa hot springs in Canada. Incidentally, rock climbers do visit from around the world to conquer the now climbable "Unclimbables." ➤

known as Big Bend, you'll begin to encounter the more sinister aspects of the Nahanni, such as Headless Creek, where the decapitated skeletons of two prospecting brothers were found in 1908. Wrote R.M. Patterson in his seminal journals exploring the region in the late 1920s: "a country lorded over by wild mountain men . . . the river fast and bad." Lured by a gold rush but forewarned of treacherous conditions, especially travelling upriver, many prospectors perished — hence the morbid place names. All of that is in contrast to the modern experience, as you drift in a protected national park reserve recognized by UNESCO as one of its four earliest World Heritage Sites. Operators such as Nahanni River Adventures make sure their clients are well fed on gourmet snacks, dozing in the twenty-two hours of daily summer sunshine as the world passes by.

After travellers bathe in the Kraus Hot Springs, the rafts gradually make their way to the islands of the Nahanni Delta, an area known as the Splits or, less kindly, Bug Hell Island. The hordes of awaiting mosquitoes are legendary, rendering bug suits essential. These are mosquitoes that take to DEET like toddlers to apple juice. But they don't seem to bother the locals in the first settlement you'll see all week, the small community of Nahanni Butte. This is where most raft journeys conclude, a welcome float plane or van waiting to return tired, sunburned, bitten, and fully inspired rafters back to civilization. Budget some time to adjust after completing one of Canada's great outdoor adventures.

START HERE: canadianbucketlist.com/nahanni

AND PINGO WAS ITS NAME-O

Bucket lists are suckers for unusual natural land formations. Atlantic Canada has its rocky flowerpots and sea arches, and western Canada its badlands hoodoos, but the North has the coolest (*ahem*) formation of them all. A pingo is a mound of frozen earth that can rise up to seventy metres high and up to six hundred metres in diameter. It's also a fun word to add to your vocabulary, coming from the Inuvialuktun word for "small hill." Alaska has the world's tallest pingo, but Tuktoyaktuk, in the Mackenzie Delta, is the best place to see these frozen upside down teacups, with 1,350 hills in the area. Pingo National Landmark protects eight of them (including Ibyuk, the world's second-tallest pingo). The pingos dominate the flat landscape here, with some being more than one thousand years old. The Inuvialuit have traditionally used the pingos as navigational landmarks or as vantage points from which to spot animals during hunts, although, due to their fragile nature, today's visitors are not allowed to walk on them. There is a boardwalk trail and viewing point at the Parks Canada–managed landmark site, with the pingos best accessed via boat tour (twenty minutes on the Beaufort Sea from Tuktoyaktuk) or a flightseeing excursion from Inuvik. Pingo!

START HERE: canadianbucketlist.com/pingo

NORTHWEST TERRITORIES ↑

ATTEND A NORTHERN FESTIVAL

Toonik Tyme, Iqaluit

Each April, as the days finally start getting longer, Iqaluit gathers for a week of games, music, and feasting. With temperatures still well below zero, the festival brings the community together, showcasing Inuit traditions and skills. Events include sealing, igloo building, dog team races, fishing, and traditional outdoor games.

Caribou Carnival, Yellowknife

Held annually since 1955, the Caribou Carnival is a celebration of life in the North, evolving from a trappers gathering into a spring celebration that attracts thousands of people from around the region.

Catch fiddle parties, survival games, and dogsled derbies, and eat off your hangover at the pancake breakfasts.

Yukon Sourdough Rendezvous, Whitehorse

With Whitehorse enduring freezing temperatures each winter, this gold rush–inspired festival is a chance to squash the cabin fever and release some energy. Participate or support competitors at the flour-packing competition, axe toss, chainsaw chuck, and log-splitting. Wisely, there are separate activities at the Kidsfest.

Dawson City Music Festival, Dawson City

A weekend music jam in 1979 has grown into one of the highlights of the Yukon summer, drawing artists from around the country to an intimate, rollicking festival. With performances taking place in multiple venues in town, the fest features family-friendly daytime programming, a New Age market, and a Midnight Dome fun run/walk.

Folk on the Rocks Festival, Yellowknife

Billed as the biggest party under the midnight sun, Yellowknife slices into summer with twenty-four hours of cultural programming on six stages, a traditional food fair, beer garden, and kids programs. There's a battle of the bands, free outdoor performances, and headline acts from northern and national artists.

Nunavut Arts Festival, Rankin Inlet

Celebrating the rich art and culture of Nunavut, this annual festival brings together the most talented artists from the territory's twenty-six incorporated communities, showcasing their talents with exhibitions, performances, and workshops.

ABOUT THOSE MOSQUITOES

They are, among many other nuisances, northern tourism's dirty little secret. *Diptera: Culicidae* is a buzz-winged, syringe-nosed space invader that attacks victims with all the tenacity of a Mongol horde (minus the civility and manners). Too small to be captured in the sweeping brochure photos of northern landscapes, mosquitoes nevertheless warrant attention because, each summer, it is a topic that sits on everybody's minds (and arms, and necks, and uncovered skin).

"Insects are only active during the brief Arctic summer, so they pack a lot of activity into their short lives," reads one of Parks Canada's welcoming booklets. Another euphemism I notice is "fierce," as in: "Mosquitoes are reliably fierce in July." It's an admirable way of saying what fierce actually means: violently hostile and aggressive, marked by unrestrained violence.

For northerners, mosquitoes are as natural as the midnight sun or northern lights (although understandably less appreciated). As with the midnight sun or northern lights, ferocious biting insects are not something most southerners have much experience with (well, us southerners who live in large, bug-free urban centres, at least). But they are certainly a wonder of the North, as in: "I wonder how many I can kill in a single hand-clap", or, "I wonder how that mosquito managed to nonchalantly fly off after I dropped a phone book on it."

Northerners have little idea how a sentence like "the rafting trip was magical, although I can't wait to get off the Benadryl for all my mosquito bites," terrifies the rest of us. Like the rare scams found in the "Danger and Annoyances" text boxes of guidebooks, we find ourselves focused less on "magical rafting trip" and more on "Benadryl." Which is a pity, because the truth is, one does make peace with the northern mosquito. We can walk out with a white flag and a big smile, and … they'll still riddle us with bite-bullets and breed on the corpses of our scabs. Still, Canadian mosquitoes are polite enough not to carry any horrible diseases like malaria. Growing up in South Africa, anti-malarial pills were a necessity for each visit to the bush, typically accompanied by harsh side effects (Lariam dreams, anyone?) and hard-to-follow dosage instructions long after the visit concluded. The first recorded case of West Nile Virus in Canada was reported in Ontario in 2002. Spread by a mosquito that has fed on an infected bird, West Nile remains extremely rare, although it does flare up every once in a while.

Some people get bitten by mosquitoes and don't get itchy (we call those people "lucky dogs"). Some people attract mosquitoes, and those unlucky dogs are great to go camping, canoeing, and hiking with. Basic mosquito precautions include long clothing and repellent or nets. Last summer I watched an Arctic mosquito bite through two layers of clothing (and a mosquito net) with all the resistance of a titanium drill entering papier-mâché. A guy on that trip slathered himself in military-grade 95 percent DEET, which would melt the innocence off a choir of schoolgirls. The usual repellent brands do suffice, which is not always the case with natural mosquito repellents. If you were to examine the mosquitoes chewing on my arm, you'd see them licking the citronella like one licks the celery-salt rim off a Caesar (both acts followed by the enthusiastic swallowing of red liquid).

But let's be serious. Bug season peaks and then settles. The initial shock of entering a cloud of bugs subsides, too. For all their annoyance, we are talking about insects that cannot stand up to a breeze. Female mosquitoes only suck our blood to nourish their eggs, so we can't blame them for wanting to be good parents. Plus, mosquitoes have played an important part in keeping Canadian wilderness as pristine and unpopulated as it is, not to mention the role they play in the pollination of Arctic flowers and feeding others higher up the food chain. A company called Oxitec has had great success with engineering a poison gene that kills breeding mosquitoes from within. Scientists believe a world without the mosquito is actually plausible, but what impact would that have on the environment? Nobody knows. As for ticking off bucket list experiences in the North, pests shouldn't stop us any more than a bad haircut. Common sense, basic precautions, perhaps a head net, and we can share the remarkable beauty of the Arctic wilderness with *all* the creatures that inhabit it — bright and beautiful, great, annoying, and small.

PERMAFROST: NOT A CHEWING GUM FLAVOUR

It sounds like a type of candyfloss, or perhaps a cool new style from a Queen Street hair salon. You'll hear permafrost mentioned quite a bit in the Arctic, so I thought I'd find out what it actually is (as opposed to what I think it is).

Soil that is frozen for two or more years is known as permafrost. It's not ice, and there doesn't necessarily need to be ice on top of it. Rather, the ground is literally frozen, as in, good-luck-trying-to-dig-a-hole frozen. Permafrost is typically covered by an "active layer" of soil that may thaw each summer. There are all sorts of wonderful geological processes going on, and if you're turned on by words like *isothermal* and *intrasedimental* and *anthropogenic*, you'll want to dig deeper (although digging in permafrost is, as we've already established, not recommended). For our purposes, it's worth noting that permafrost contains 1,700 billion tons of organic matter, a.k.a. carbon, which would cause 1,700 billion tons of havoc were it all released in the atmosphere. One group of scientists believe a global temperature rise of just 1.5°C would thaw the permafrost in Siberia, which sounds boring but is probably really important. In the Arctic, you'll notice that buildings above permafrost are built on piles so they don't sink into the thawing ground, with utility lines, pipes, and cables all located aboveground. Permafrost is also a great refrigerator, from whence we have obtained well-preserved fossils, bones, and other evidence of extinct polar animals.

HOOK A NORTHERN PIKE

Life is too short not to do what you're passionate about, which in Carlos Gonzalez's case is fishing, cooking, and introducing visitors from around the world to the beauty and bounty of Great Slave Lake. His log cabins rest on its shores, his boats zip about its rocky islands, and Carlos loves nothing more than catching-and-releasing the prize trophy in the world's ninth-largest lake, the great northern pike.

Great Slave (the name has nothing to do with slavery, but is attributed to the Slavey First Nation) covers an area of 27,000 square kilometres, a very big lake for very big fish. The largest of them all, sitting at the top of its underwater food chain, is the great northern pike. Dark green with yellow spots, they can grow up to 1.5 metres, weigh as much as thirty kilos, and are prized by sport fishers for their

Freedom on Great Slave Lake

It's certainly not the most digestible name for a lake, but you can relax: Great Slave Lake has nothing to do with slavery. *Slave*, in this case, should be pronounced *Slavey*, after the indigenous people who lived there when English explorer Samuel Hearne stumbled upon the lake in 1771. It is fed by Slave River, which should also consider adding an accurate and innocuous *y* to its name. ➤

aggressive, fighting nature. With teeth as sharp as sharks, northern pike (also known as jackfish) patrol the waters preying on trout, whitefish, and other unlucky creatures. Over the years, Carlos has seen some monsters, but he runs a strict catch-and-release operation. Such is his respect for the pike that if someone is after a trophy, he's happy to lose the revenue.

Kitted out in rain gear, we speedboat out of his base in Yellowknife's Old Town. Backs to the wind, Carlos manoeuvres us through the dozens of islands that dot the north arm of Great Slave. It's easy to see how treacherous these channels can be, the shallow rocks lurking beneath the waters like predators. After forty-five minutes, he finds a quiet spot, hands our small group some rods, and instructs us how to cast, reel and jerk for pike. There's no time to sit back and drink beers. We stand on one side of the boat, repeatedly casting our lines, with no bait and a single hook. Within minutes, Jason from Korea snags a beauty! "That's Emily," says Carlos, holding the fish up so Jason can pose for photographs. No sooner has he released the fish back into the water than my dad snags his first of the day, introduced by Carlos as "George." Next up is Jennifer, Samuel (my first catch), and Big Bertha, a beast of a beauty, about one metre in length. By the time we break for lunch, we have caught and released a total of eight pikes, have let a dozen get away, and are well satisfied with our accomplishments.

Fishing is only half the fun. With his background in restaurants, Carlos takes shore lunches seriously. Although he has picnic tables and firepits on various islands, we head to the comfort of the warm, fully stocked cabin for a barbecue of lake trout marinated in olive oil, basil, garlic, and lemon fusion.

"Some friends of mine amassed small fortunes, and always said they'd do things when they retired, but then they started dropping dead, literally," says Carlos. What's it all for if you're not doing what you want with it? From a small fishing operation set up in 1991 to keep him busy during the summers, his Yellowknife Outdoor Adventures has grown into one of the region's top outfitters, offering aurora viewing at the cabin, snowmobile adventures, and trips to Nahanni National Park. Having moved north from Montreal thirty years ago to "escape the traffic," he's clearly enjoying himself — and so are we.

The biggest fish I've ever caught, on one of the most spectacular lakes I've ever seen. Now that's one for the bucket list.

START HERE: canadianbucketlist.com/pike

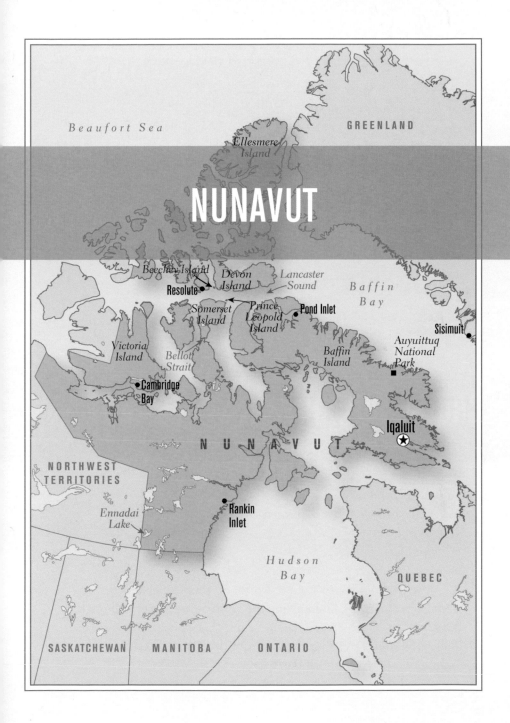

NUNAVUT

Beaufort Sea

GREENLAND

Ellesmere
Island

Beechey Island
Resolute
Devon
Island
Lancaster
Sound
Baffin
Bay
Somerset
Island
Prince
Leopold
Island
Pond Inlet
Sisimuit
Victoria
Island
Bellot
Strait
Baffin
Island
Auyuittuq
National
Park
Cambridge
Bay

N U N A V U T

Iqaluit

NORTHWEST
TERRITORIES

Ennadai
Lake

Rankin
Inlet

Hudson
Bay

QUEBEC

SASKATCHEWAN
MANITOBA
ONTARIO

CRUISE THE NORTHWEST PASSAGE

In those Northwest Voyages
Where navigation must be executed
In exquisite sort.
— John Davis, 1594

It suspends from the roof of the world, an intricate chandelier of a frozen archipelago, illuminating the wind-burned faces of those in search of adventure. A desolate landscape of ice and rock that, nevertheless, promises wealth and glory, and, like any light burning too bright, doom for those that don't pay heed. The Northwest Passage connects Europe and Asia across the Arctic. A safe, reliable passage

could double the speed and halve the cost of traditional shipping routes. Explorers of legend first sailed in search of its discovery as early as the sixteenth century, finding themselves in a forbidding and unpredictable polar wasteland, home to strange creatures, curious natives, desolate storms, and labyrinthine icy passages trapping boats like bugs in a spider's web. It didn't stop them coming, sea dog captains whose names we still recall hundreds of years later. Frobisher Bay, Davis Strait, McClintock Channel, Baffin Island, Fort Ross — legends of Arctic exploration, and yet the most famous of all has no great islands or bays named after him. Sir John Franklin even casts a shadow over the first man who successfully found his way through, the Norwegian Roald Amundsen. The fate of Franklin's Expedition (see page 89) remains a mystery, the scarred and scattered bones found on several islands suggesting foul depths of human misery. Today, from the comfort of an ice-strengthened expedition ship, we can follow Franklin's footsteps, at least to the point where they fade away.

Anyone can attempt the Northwest Passage now in a manner of comfort early explorers could never have imagined. Attracting

passengers from around the world, some of us are here for the history, others for the landscape and wildlife. All are aware that we are embarking on a true northern adventure into an astonishing part of the world that very few people will ever see. Bundle up, bucket listers. Bring your cameras, your books, and your appetite for curiosity. The charter flight from Ottawa to Kangerlussuaq, Greenland, is taxiing down the runway. Awaiting us is One Ocean Expedition's 117-metre-long, eighteen-metre-wide *Akademik Sergey Vavilov*. Awaiting us is a once-in-a-lifetime Arctic adventure.

Eighty-four passengers, sixty-six crew, ten Zodiacs, and almost two thousand nautical miles to sail in twelve days if we hope to return home via a charter flight from Cambridge Bay to Edmonton. We begin in Greenland, the world's biggest island and the least densely populated country in the world, because Franklin's final voyage passed through here, too, filling up on supplies and sending five unfit (but ultimately lucky) men home before the ships crossed Baffin Bay and promptly vanished. A thick ice-sheet blankets most of Greenland, with a small, primarily Inuit population clinging to the narrow shorelines. There is not a tree to be found anywhere, but farther up the coast, in the town of Sisimiut, it is anything but drab. Houses are painted bright colours, modern supermarkets sell fresh produce, and locals are stylishly Scandinavian, as befits a nation still officially governed by Denmark.

Life in Greenland is distinctly different from life in the Canadian Arctic, even though culturally the Inuit communities are similar. As we wander the town, finding healthy Icelandic horses grazing in a field of Arctic poppies and dozens of boisterous barking huskies, the passengers sniff each other out. There is a large group from the Vancouver Aquarium, media from New York and Germany, a museum director who happens to have been the last Canadian to circumnavigate North America, scientists, artists, photographers, writers, families, couples, and, of course, travellers, like yourself.

More than just a cruise ship, the *Vavilov* will conduct important Arctic research, transform into a floating museum, host presentations and exhibits that include original maps from the 1850s and relics from the recently discovered *Erebus* (see page 90). We are, after all, on the same vessel that was instrumental in the discovery of Franklin's flagship in September 2014. While One Ocean staff is comprised of cheery North Americans, the ship's working crew is Russian, our rooms basic yet comfortable. Meals are outstanding; a Scotch bar is well-stocked, fine wine will flow. There's a Finnish sauna and a hot tub on the upper deck. But if you're thinking a glitzy floating hotel can take on the Northwest Passage, think again. Due to heavy sea ice and prowling icebergs, there's no guarantee that even our expedition ship will make it. This is a journey of discovery on the icy fringes of adventure tourism. When the highlights include grave markers of dead sailors on one of the bleakest islands you can imagine, nobody is here for the tan and Jimmy Buffett's "Margaritaville."

Crossing the Davis Strait north toward Baffin Island brings monstrous ten-thousand- year-old icebergs, lurking for unsuspecting boat hulls and maritime disasters. We take the Zodiacs into a jigsaw puzzle of glacial ice and cruise about this frozen sculpture garden, admiring the formations and alien-blue colours, the seabirds standing guard atop each berg like sentinels. Icebergs in the shape of sea dragons and ducks, archways, mushrooms, flowerpots, plateaus, wedges, and a five-storey crown for Poseidon's head. So many shapes, and this just the *tip* of a proverbial metaphor!

From the ship's bridge, a quiet, serious place that is nonetheless open to passengers, I watch the *Vavilov* cautiously push aside growlers and dense, heart-of-glacier black ice. This is an ice-strengthened vessel, not an icebreaker. Fortunately, a high-pressure zone has calmed the seas for our two-day ocean crossing. Fascinating presentations about Franklin, marine biology, life in the Arctic and beyond keep us busy. When a polar bear is spotted on some sea ice many miles from shore, I understand why *Ursus maritimus* is classified as a marine mammal.

Beyond the staggering views and intriguing history, any Northwest Passage crossing is a journey of people — the passengers who share meals and excursions and late nights at the bar, the people of the Arctic we encounter in remote northern towns like Pond Inlet. Residents here demonstrate their sport, throat singing, dancing, and drumming at the Cultural Centre. I ask one of them what she thinks about us tourists arriving en masse.

"It's a little like a human zoo," she tells me. "We get to see people from all over the world."

"Wait a second," I ask. "You mean, *we* are the ones in the cage?"

"Of course!" She laughs. The Inuit sense of humour is legendary.

Harsh realities are never too far away in the Arctic. We discover during our brief visit that a local family have been seriously injured

in a tent fire. Without a resident doctor in Pond Inlet, our ship doctor, Thandi Wilkinson, rushes to help. She spends the next twelve hours frantically trying to save lives, making national news in the process, and receiving a formal letter of gratitude from the Nunavut government. Guests are more than willing to halt our itinerary and put the lives of strangers first. One Ocean's polar commitment to leave only footprints transcends environmental responsibility. It extends to Arctic communities, too.

Later, a shore excursion at Dundas Harbour on Devon Island shows us just how far those communities stretch into the past. Hiking along the coastline, we encounter the remains of an RCMP camp from the 1920s, sunken stones from five-hundred-year-old Thule settlements, and evidence of the Dorsets, who colonized the central and eastern Arctic two millenniums ago. Highlighter-orange lichen, lime-green mosses, and yellow poppies thrive in the sunshine. Light this far north has a rejuvenating quality, as if Mother Nature has just learned Photoshop. Some life, yes, but death is never far behind. The landscape becomes a rocky desert, leading up to the almost century-old graves of two RCMP offers, overlooking a barren bay. As we sail farther into Lancaster Sound, the surrounding islands exude an alien starkness. No wonder NASA tested its Mars Rover on Devon Island.

"The chewed bones of Franklin's men are rolling in the perma-frost," I tell some new friends as we blissfully drink beer in *Vavilov's* upper deck hot tub. We have just sailed past the most spectacular iceberg I've ever seen, its two blue-ice peaks shimmering, taller than the ship. The more we learn about the tribulations of early Arctic explorers, the more we become aware of the ship's comforts, from the cappuccino machine, infused cocktails, and reading lamps to the onboard massage therapist. Despite the modern technology, the

GPS and radar and stabilizers, ships still sink or get grounded in the Northwest Passage. The seriousness of the officers in the bridge is reassuring, even if our Russian captain's real name, and I'm not making this up, is Captain Valeriy Beluga.

Visitors to Beechey Island feel Arctic frost pile up on their bones. The Franklin expedition overwintered on this small spit of an island, as bleak a frozen wasteland as you'd ever want to visit. Case in point: wooden grave markers where three of Franklin's men are buried. When the bodies were exhumed for study in the 1980s, the death mask of twenty-year-old John Torrington made world news, giving a twelve-year-old boy in South Africa nightmares. Twenty-five years later, I'm standing above the permafrost-preserved grave of Torrington, and I still can't get his blonde locks, peeled eyelids, and shrunken lips out of my head. Survival suits, provided to all *Vavilov* passengers for each excursion, may be designed for the elements but are vulnerable to thoughts of desperate men boiling human bones to suck out the marrow. Real-life horror blows icy chills down your neck, no matter what you're wearing. We walk up the rocky beach to memorial cairns, finding rusted tins discarded from unsuccessful rescue missions. Beechey Island doesn't even feature in the Atlas back in the ship's library. For

those on the trail of Franklin, its significance is undeniable.

There is no web access on the *Vavilov*. No world news, no Facebook, no email. It adds to the sense of isolation, our removal from work, loved ones, and the rest of wired-up humanity. When the ship repositions alongside the imposing table-flat cliffs of Prince Leopold Island, it feels like we've entered a location in a fantasy novel. The seasonal home for hundreds of thousands of migratory birds, it looks as if the ghost of Jackson Pollock splattered white streaks of guano on the almost one-thousand-foot-high limestone cliffs.

Despite the impressive array of camera lenses onboard, nobody's gotten a great picture of a whale yet. Marine mammals continue to be frustratingly scarce. Fortunately, nobody got a photo of me slipping off the outdoor stairway on the stern either. Making my way from the hot tub to the sauna, I found myself spread-eagled on the cold metal, bruised and bashed but miraculously in one piece. It hurt to laugh, but laugh I did. Would Parry, Amundsen, or the mighty John Rae have been impressed that I'd somehow managed to clutch onto the can of Heineken? I make a joke to a nearby Russian sailor that my meat had been tenderized. Given the history of cannibalism in the Arctic, I don't think he found it funny.

If there's a climax when crossing the Northwest Passage, we find it in the Bellot Strait. A hairline fracture on a map, just under a kilometre wide at its narrowest point, our evening crossing must be perfectly timed to stem the tide. With the Arctic sun sparkling on lake-smooth

Tony Soper co-founded BBC's Natural History Unit, produced and hosted numerous wildlife TV shows, and penned bestselling guidebooks about the Arctic and Northwest Passage. Having crossed the passage eight times, I asked this avid birder about his highlight:

"Polar bears patrol the Northwest Passage but birders will be looking for them in the hope of seeing a rare gull in close company. Ivory gulls are confined to Arctic latitudes. Slightly larger than common kittiwakes but better designed for life in the harsh icescape, they long ago reduced the webs between their toes to reduce heat loss and curved their claws to improve grip on the ice. They hang around settlements in the hope of handouts or follow dog teams for scraps. Mostly though, they specialize in following polar bears to take advantage of the flesh and blubber that litter a killing ground. Whiter than white, these ethereal birds are master scavengers." ➤

water, the Atlantic finally meets the Pacific. On our left (port side) is the northernmost point of continental North America, on the right (starboard) is the first land forms of the Arctic Archipelago. Two polar bears swim alongside either side of us, cutting a triangle wake in the calm water. Seals swim up ahead and we get swept up in the moment, some of us singing with the ghost of Stan Rogers, others eating hot blueberry crumble gratefully brought to the frigid upper deck. I have cruised around the Galapagos, Antarctica, and in the Caribbean and South China Seas. Crossing the Bellot Strait under a midnight sun on a clear, icy evening is as memorable an ocean experience as one can have.

"Em, I think that bear is eating a beluga whale!"

Our Zodiacs are invading Conningham Bay on the eastern shore of Prince Edward Island (the Arctic version, not the Maritimes one). Skirting through sea ice, two large adult male bears are feasting on

five baby belugas, the bears comfortable with our presence as we gently drift toward them in muted silence. Shallow waters in the bay often trap belugas when the tide recedes, resulting in a buffet for local hunters and hungry bears. A large snowy owl gazes down on us as our Zodiacs putter deeper into the bay, encountering more than a dozen young belugas that survived the tide. The Arctic is not the Serengeti. Animals that live north of 66 degrees are hunted, and therefore skittish. As rare as wildlife encounters may be, there's a purity in the moment, the triumph of having worked for it, even if the wind is cold enough to strip the paint off a Zamboni.

A century after Amundsen, and sixty years after Canada's St. Roche found the first deep-water Northwest Passage, less than three hundred registered ships have successfully navigated the Northwest Passage. Is our crossing with the *Vavilov* among them? Some might argue our east to west passage doesn't count, that we didn't travel from Baffin Bay to the Beaufort Sea.

"I think you can legitimately call it the Northwest Passage. It's nitpicking to say our trip didn't cover the critical stuff, [that] we've done the best bits." This from the mouth of Tony Sopar, an Arctic legend who has sailed the passage eight times, and written the region's bestselling guidebooks. He's aboard with us, too, along with so many wonderful people who have once again demonstrated that any passage is only as meaningful as the people you share it with. Eating the muktuk (this time, raw narwhal) that Graydon procured in Greenland, learning how to smile with my eyes from Leslie, our onboard Inuit interpreter, the Scots teaching me about Scotch, the aquarium folks about marine conservation, the photographers how to frame a good story. Everyone has a warm story to share. Canadians, Australians, Americans, Brits, Germans, Russians, and Dutch ... there are cruise ships, expedition ships, battleships, and cargo ships, but every sailor worth his or her salt knows the most important of them all are friendships. Forgive me there if I went overboard with the sentimentality.

For all the history, there's murkiness when it comes to the future of the Arctic. Climate change is leading to potential ice-free summers, and with the possibility of a reliable passage revolutionizing the shipping industry, nations are sharpening their claws and planting their flags. As for the opportunity to explore the Northwest Passage onboard One Ocean's *Akademik Sergey Vavilov*? No murkiness about this one. It's a bucket list experience as clear as ice.

START HERE: canadianbucketlist.com/northwestpassage

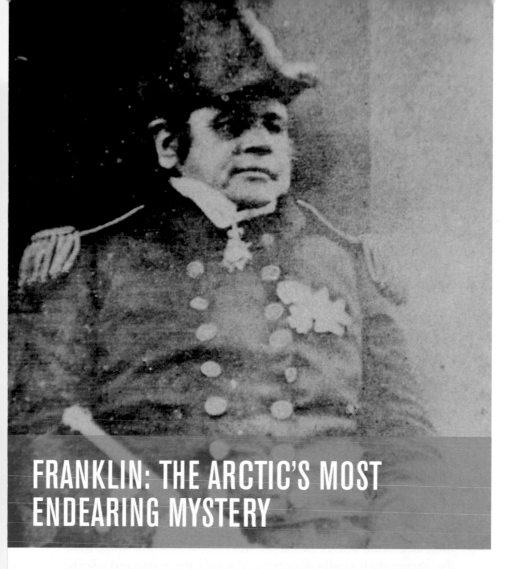

FRANKLIN: THE ARCTIC'S MOST ENDEARING MYSTERY

It is one of the greatest and most shocking of all maritime mysteries. How did two ice-strengthened ships, captained by polar veterans and stocked with the latest and greatest in shipping technology, vanish into the ice of the Northwest Passage, with all 129 men on board? From the moment the expedition left England in May 1845, the fate of the Royal Navy bomb vessels *Erebus* and *Terror* has captured the public imagination.

Franklin, a controversial choice to command the expedition, was widely seen as being too old for the challenge ahead. His notoriety today has more to do with his wife Lady Jane Franklin's

SEE UNICORNS FROM THE ICE FLOE

The jury is still out on why an Arctic whale sprouts a long, spiral tusk more familiar from fantasy posters of unicorns. More certain is the fact that the tusk of the narwhal inspired the mythical unicorn. A rare and prized whale found only in the Arctic, some historians believe that whalers deliberately withheld information about the narwhal in order to increase the value and mystery of its long, spiral tusk. Primarily found in males, the tusk typically extrudes from the upper left canine, and can grow up to three metres in length. Marine scientists still don't know what purpose the tusk fulfils, although it is generally believed to distinguish males for mating purposes. There is no evidence that narwhal hunt or fend off predators with the protrusions.

The trade of unicorn horn is tightly regulated in Canada and illegal in the United States, but it is perfectly acceptable and you are

thoroughly encouraged to visit Pond Inlet, connect with an operator like Co-op Outfitting or Tagak Outfitting, and head out to the floe edge to see this remarkable creature in action. If the weather co-operates, it's about a two-hour snowmobile ride on the sea ice. Finding leads in the ice during the spring months, narwhal families (some of them up to one thousand strong) swim north in search of rich marine feeding grounds. While you're in Pond Inlet, contact the local Parks Canada office to arrange a visit to the stunning glaciers and migratory bird sanctuary in Sirmilik National Park.

VISIT THE WORLD'S MOST NORTHERLY ECO-LODGE

Arctic Sunwest Charters's de Havilland Dash 8 takes off from Yellowknife on the 1,500-kilometre journey north into the neighbouring territory of Nunavut. On board are tourists from Connecticut, New Mexico, Scotland, New York, and California, along with a group of Canadian geologists and some marine scientists from Mystic Aquarium. Our destination is Arctic Watch, a unique beluga whale observation post and eco-lodge located eight hundred kilometres north of the Arctic Circle.

As a launch pad for a once-in-a-lifetime Arctic safari, the Watch boasts several attractions: the most comfortable remote facilities in the High Arctic (private tented cabins, gourmet meals, Internet), a variety of tundra toys, an impeccable location, and the fact that it is owned and operated by Richard Weber and his family. Weber is the most travelled North Pole explorer on the planet, the first man to trek to the North Pole six times, including unsupported expeditions that have never been equalled. His wife, Josée, has led six expeditions herself, and both have also trekked to the South Pole (Richard kite-sledded out). Both sons are in the business as well: Tessum holds the distinction of being the youngest person to trek to the North Pole, while Nansen is an accomplished wildlife photographer. These are people who live and love the Arctic, sharing this passion with others at their summer camp overlooking the purple inlet of the Cunningham River. During the short summer months, when the sun burns twenty-four hours a day, a charter flight lands once a week on the tundra runway. It switches over the week's guests, bringing with it a load of fresh food and supplies. I'm as north as I've ever been, nigh an elf toss from Santa. The desolate tundra looks like the moon, and fittingly, a moon buggy is waiting to greet us.

WATCH BELUGAS PLAY AT YOUR FEET

Our group piles into the back of a bright yellow Unimog, a fifty-year-old four-by-four truck that somehow weathers one of the harshest climates on the planet. It's a short drive to the lodge, comprising a large dome-shaped communal dining tent, bathrooms, and hot showers, a fully equipped restaurant-grade kitchen, and an equipment room. Adjacent individual living quarters, with double beds, sinks, and marine toilets, sit outside like milk chocolate Hershey kisses. Every summer, up to two thousand beluga whales gather at the mouth of the Cunningham River for a natural body wash and to feed on rich nutrients in the flowing Arctic meltwaters. We excitedly put on rubber boots and walk over the rock and estuaries to the river mouth, drawn to the water boiling with life up ahead.

We're in luck: ice at the mouth of the inlet has finally cleared and the whales have arrived, hundreds of them, arching their backs, popping their heads out of the water, rolling and rubbing their bodies on the gravel below. Belugas, among the most social of all whales, cackle and chirp with delight as marine scientists tell us their exfoliating gravel skin rub is actually pleasurable. I can almost hear David Attenborough's voice narrating the phenomenon of these Arctic ghosts, and you can if you watch BBC's *Frozen Planet*, which filmed a beluga segment right here at Arctic Watch. Fittingly, it turns out that two of the guys on my plane are actually BBC nature filmmakers. I love nature documentaries and often wonder: "Where in the world is that?" What a remarkable feeling when you realize *that* is right in front of you.

SLEEP UNDER THE MIDNIGHT SUN

Considering the nearest grocery store is 1,500 kilometres away, chef Jeff Stewart and the staff serve up magnificent fare: roast lamb, braised ribs, pickled Arctic char, adobo chicken, butter-smooth tenderloin, fresh salads, and vegetables. There is homemade bread, mayonnaise, and yogurt. Much like my experience at Skokie Lodge (Banff), I'm eating like royalty in the wilderness.

We're introduced to the Webers and the young, attractive staff. It's easy to make yourself at home when it feels like a home, complete with Josée, the nurturing mom. Our groups span a wide range of ages (eight to seventy) and interests (birders, scientists, hikers, photographers), and the Watch does its best to make sure everyone is accommodated. We're chatting in the main lodge, getting to know one another, when I make two rather dumb comments:

What not to say in the High Arctic summer, Part 1: **Damn, I just realized I forgot my headlamp!**

What not to say in the High Arctic summer, Part 2: **Wow, we're so remote, the stars are going to be epic tonight!**

There are no stars, of course, for the same reason I won't need to worry about a flashlight. This far north, the sun wheels across the sky, roughly fifteen degrees every fifteen minutes. It never sets, and so the sky never so much as gets mildly dusky. The midnight sun is disorienting but energizing. Still, with the white fabric of our sleeping tents, I quickly realize:

What not to say in the High Arctic summer, Part 3: **I forgot my eye mask!**

The comfortable beds have heavy duvets and warm fleece sheets. Yet high winds shake the tents, and polar bears stalk my dreams. I awake constantly on my first night, panicking that I've overslept for the morning's activities. It's okay, it's only two a.m., bright as day. Sleeping without night is an early afternoon nap that never ends.

SWIM IN AN ARCTIC WATERFALL

Tessum Weber greets me with a freshly made cappuccino in the morning. Each day, the youngest man to trek to the North Pole is my personal barista. After a hearty breakfast, we go for a walk to some local waterfalls. The tundra is sweeping, a desert of shale skipping stones and crushed limestone — desert, that is, were it not for the bright blue streams, mineralized with rock flour into shades of green and turquoise. The local waterfall is a fifteen-metre beauty, surrounded by sharp-cut canyon walls. Farther up, a series of smaller but just as striking cascades invite a swim. If God put us on Earth to endure supermarket lineups and mortgages, He wanted us to take Arctic waterfall showers too.

I strip down and take a refreshing dip in water pure enough to bottle and sell to Fiji. Thanks to warming temperatures and shrinking Arctic ice, mosquitoes have invaded the island for the first time. They're as big as oil rigs, ready to drill, but fortunately, their small numbers are nothing compared with bug net hell down south.

We continue our walk, familiarizing ourselves with the landscape. Although the island is covered in a sheet of ice for much of the year, life stubbornly resists in the form of small plants, flowers, and white candy balls of Arctic cotton. We walk through a valley, giving a wide berth to a sandpiper protecting her nest. A hot lunch awaits, the ATVs are fuelled, and there just might be a larger form of life lurking sixteen kilometres away, at Polar Bear Point.

Five Arctic Creatures that Turn White for Winter

For greater warmth and protection against predators, animals in the Arctic go through a remarkable transformation in the winter.

Arctic hare: brown and black during summer months
ermine: world's smallest weasel flips brown to white
Arctic fox: nature's most northerly fox is brown-grey in summer
barren ground caribou: predominantly brown in summer, predominantly white in winter
rock ptarmigan: moults brown to white in winter, keeping its brown or black tail

ATV TO ICEBERGS AND ANCIENT RUINS

The Watch is as small as a poppy seed on a basketball court. To get around, we'd need the Unimog, rafts, and tough ATVs built for such terrain. I salute our opposable thumbs, which gave humanity the dexterity to evolve beyond the apes, build tools, text message, and accelerate on ATVs.

We drive up along the coast, crossing streams and crunching rocks, past an old scientific observation cabin and slowly towards the famed Northwest Passage. The path is lined by inukshuks, piled stones used by Inuit for millennia as a form of communication and

guidance. The stone guardians ensure we are travelling in the right direction. In the distance are icebergs, along with floating crusts of slowly melting sea ice.

Tessum stops off at a small circular mound of rocks, explaining that these are the archaeological remains of thousand-year-old Thule hunting stations. Dozens of similar stations line the coast, where Inuit ancestors hunted whales and seals. We can still see the heavy bones of bowhead and beluga whales. I tell Tessum I've seen UNESCO World Heritage Site status awarded for less, but he says such remains are fairly common up the coast, where many of the stations have not been excavated.

We continue to the point, racing along the beach, slaloming between beached chunks of ice. Two large icebergs are drifting just offshore. We stop to observe the ice, hopping between the giant floating slabs. Steve from Santa Fe spots something through his binoculars, and sure enough, it's a polar bear. One of the staff always

carries a rifle, just in case, and we're given bear spray in case we decide to wander off. But since the lodge opened in 2000, there has never been any problem with the bears. In fact, in all of Richard Weber's expeditions to the North Pole, he has never even seen a bear, although he has come across their tracks. They're out there, but with this much space, no two species have to cramp each other's style.

HIKE IN THE TUNDRA

Eight thousand years ago, the vast plains of the tundra that buttress Cunningham Inlet were under the sea. We can see this as we hike among the fossils and shells on its distinctly seabed landscape. Once past the rocks that have been gathered downstream by the river, the ground becomes soft and spongy with moss, sprouting tufts of grass like hair on the face of a teenage boy. A finger-thick branch of Arctic willow, growing low to the soil, might be a century old. Only the hardiest of life can survive here. Alpine sorrel (with leaves that taste like strawberry), Arctic poppies, and glossy yellow buttercups whisper a fragile beauty in this unforgiving starkness.

We hike along the blue river that cuts through Gull Canyon, spotting boisterous Arctic hares on the mossy green slopes. There's no need to carry a water bottle; we simply drink from the streams. Mucks, the insulated rubber boot of choice at Arctic Watch, prove

An Ode to My Mucks

You keep my feet warm and dry
Your weight in gold one cannot deny
Crossing streams and mud, moss, and gravel
Without you, my piggies unravel!
My Arctic boot, my rubber soul
Let's take this tundra, es-rock and roll!

invaluable across this terrain. At one point they magically keep water out after a river crossing that went up to my knees. I haven't had such appreciation for a product since I discovered the iPod.

We walk to Sunday Lake ("because we used to visit here on Sundays," explains Josée) across a badlands landscape, discovering the scattered remains of bowhead whales miles inshore. Arctic fox cubs were spotted in a nearby den a few weeks ago, but today it is abandoned. The white skull of a baby fox on the tundra is a reminder that life is tough in the wild, and only the strongest survive. We walk past more bones. "Members of the Franklin expedition?" I joke, recalling the ill-fated British mission to discover the Northwest Passage, a mission that scattered the frozen, scurvied, and emaciated remains of 129 men throughout the region.

A strong, biting breeze is picking up, so we return to the Watch, appreciating the hot roasted veggies and sweet desserts more than ever. Some primeval instinct has given me a huge appetite, as if it expects no further supply planes to arrive.

PADDLE A CRYSTAL CLEAR ARCTIC STREAM

Canada is baking in a mid-July heat wave, but the Arctic turns on us. Gale force winds rock our tents, stinging rain attacks the windows of the lodge, as the temperature plummets and snow begins to fall. We huddle up with coffee and hot chocolate in the lodge as the Mystic marine scientists give a presentation about beluga behaviour and Richard Weber takes us on a journey to the North Pole.

Having received numerous awards and honours, no less than Sir Ranulph Fiennes has called Richard, and his partner Misha Malakhov, the "greatest of all Arctic travellers." Listening to tales of his military-like preparation and experience is fascinating, a battle against the harshest elements on the planet. The keys to his success are efficiency, the right caloric intake, walking distances, body-fat

ratio, gear, equipment, and attitude. His words are efficient, too, an Arctic general with no time or energy to waste.

Next up, Jeff Turner and Justin Maguire show us an Attenborough-narrated BBC documentary they filmed in British Columbia. They captured wolves attacking a grizzly, and spent months waiting for those jaw-dropping shots you see on TV. One guest is a bestselling photographer, another a bond trader obsessed with great migrations. Everyone is having a bucket list sort of week.

Although it's still chilly and grey, by the following day the weather has softened enough to allow us to head upstream on the Unimog to meet river rafts and a kayak. The river is as smooth as glass, so after a lunch in the field (heartwarming borscht) I hop in the kayak with a Belarusian named Rus and expertly snap the steering pedal. We head over some gentle rapids backwards, but the current is generous and smooth, and so, straightening up, it shepherds us along the canyon under the watchful gaze of a rough-legged hawk. The others follow us in the rafts, berthing on the gravel after someone spots a muskox. Although they've been hunted for their fur and meat, today we stalk these shaggy beasts of the tundra with our cameras.

With another storm blowing in, we retreat to base, where the brave decide to bear the icy winds to spend more time with the belugas. I opt for beluga-shaped ice cubes in a glass of Iceberg vodka with a teaspoon of honey. It keeps the Arctic chill at bay.

FISH FOR ARCTIC CHAR

Freezing rain or shine, there is one day left to head deeper into the tundra, on rugged Bombardier all-terrain vehicles. I've ridden ATVs before, but never on a landscape so complementary to their capabilities: muddy, rocky, wet, no trees for thousands of kilometres. Warned never to underestimate the Arctic, I layered up to the point of absurdity (three pairs of socks, two layers of merino wool long underwear). Our destination, Inukshuk Lake, is a three-hour ride away, where we will pull out rods and attempt to catch some tasty Arctic char. Similar to salmon, Arctic char is lighter, whiter, and rarer to find on your plate.

Just minutes outside the Watch, I'm once again feeling the isolation, desolation, and striking beauty of the tundra. We cross rivers and estuaries, and ride on the spines of ridges, even as a light snow begins to fall. Tessum stops up ahead and points out two muskox in the valley below. They appear to be running toward us, disappearing on the slope before popping up thirty metres away. They're not snorting or stamping their feet, but it's unusual for these huge Arctic creatures to get so close. They trot along onto the path in front of us, and for the next ten minutes they clear our way, like squad cars leading a motorcade. Finally they vanish into a valley below, leaving us elated from the encounter.

After roller-coastering up and down muddy banks and rocky hills, we arrive at the lake. Low cloud hovers on the hills, draining all colour. Then the sun breaks through for a moment, pouring turquoise dye into the water. Sven and Tessum prepare the rods, and after soup, sandwiches, and coffee we're casting our lines from the shore. Landlocked char grow slowly, and a strict quota is in place. Our goal is to catch four medium-sized fish for the kitchen and catch-and-release the rest. It's Sven, Arctic Watch's shaggy-haired handyman, who reels in the first couple of char. As for me, let's just say if you teach this man to fish, he's still not going to catch anything.

On the long ride back (when did you last spend six hours on an ATV?), with my right thumb on the throttle, I find myself zoning out. Life seems very simple: get back to the warmth of the Watch, eat, survive. This is the way of the Arctic north.

Considering its size, I explored but a fraction's fraction of Nunavut. I did not get the opportunity to spend time with its Inuit people, nor to visit their towns and settlements. Yet as small as my Arctic dosage was, it was in the company of people who love it, explore it, and are devoted to introducing us southerners to its wonders. Nunavut before you die? You'd be a macadamia not to.

START HERE: canadianbucketlist.com/arcticwatch

PAINT THE ARCTIC

Cory Trépanier is a well-known artist and filmmaker with a passion for capturing the Canadian wilderness on canvas. He has spent more than a decade developing his *Into the Arctic* collection of oil paintings, developed from four expeditions to some of the most remote corners of the Arctic. Immersing himself into the landscape and travelling via foot, canoe, plane, and boat, his adventures in the North have produced a travelling museum exhibition of seventy-five paintings, three documentary films, and global awareness for the wonders of the Arctic.

Q: You're originally from Windsor, Ontario. What attracted a southern Ontario boy to the North?

A: The desire to paint the wildest and most untouched landscapes in Canada. I was originally inspired by our Heritage rivers, some of which flowed north to the Arctic. It opened my horizons with its vastness, and a landscape so different from anything I'd ever painted before. A beautiful part of the world so few people had ever seen.

Q: You're actually painting on site, in the elements. A little different from a traditional studio setting, I imagine?

A: Totally. The reason for doing this is to experience the landscape on an emotional level, laying down the foundation so that the final painting, completed in the studio, has a better chance of conveying what I'm feeling when I'm out there. It makes the challenges worthwhile, which include mosquitoes trying to gnaw me to the bone, freezing temperatures, strong winds, rain, polar bears, you know … the usual studio challenges!

Q: So what belongs on every Canadian's Northern Bucket List?

A: Wilberforce Falls west of Bathurst Inlet is higher than Niagara Falls, and the most beautiful falls in the Arctic, plunging into an incredible red-lined canyon. Coronation Fjord in Auyuittuq National Park is a three- to four-kilometre glacier with kilometre-high cliffs on either side, with the spectacular Penny Ice Cap in the background. I found a view on Banks Island in Aulavik National Park that took my breath away, wishing I had a much larger canvas. I hope my paintings inspire others with the beauty of the North, but hopefully they will have a greater desire to experience it for themselves.

Q: Not too many people get the opportunity to visit these spots. What advice can you give those who are interested?

A: It can be challenging getting to the North, but there are companies

that create accessible Arctic experiences, across a wide range of comfort levels. Some people might choose to do backcountry trips in our amazing national parks; others can look to operators like One Ocean Expeditions, Arctic Kingdom, or Black Feather. However you choose to do it, any trip into the Arctic creates experiences and memories that will stay with you for the rest of your life.

You can check out Cory's paintings at trepanieroriginals.com and his Arctic adventures at intothearctic.ca.

BUILD AN ARCTIC KINGDOM

Graham Dickson is the founder of Arctic Kingdom Polar Expeditions (arctickingdom.com), having led more than fifty polar expeditions for adventurers, scientists, TV crews, tourists, and divers. He's dived with walrus, narwhal, belugas, and the enormous Greenland sharks, and he led the first ice-climbing expedition to scale icebergs in Nunavut. Arctic Kingdom offers a range of bucket list backcountry Arctic adventures, wildlife safaris, and diving excursions. I caught up with Graham via satellite in remote Baffin Island:

Q: In the chase for one-of-a-kind adventures, why should people think North? What makes it different from other places in Canada?

A: The Arctic is Canada's third seacoast, and the location of animal migrations that rival those of the African plains. Narwhal and caribou move from winter ranges to summer ranges. Polar bear and ring seals follow the ice.

Q: Diving in the North sounds surreal? What can one expect — and wait, isn't it freezing?

A: I've been diving in the North since 1999. I admit it isn't tropical, but with the right gear, divers are comfortable. Our Baffin Island Dive Safari coincides with the annual migration of narwhal — the single-tusked whale that was the inspiration for unicorn legends. The sea ice has not completely melted, so we can dive near icebergs frozen in place. Underwater photography opportunities are amazing.

Q: Wildlife can be scarce in a region as vast as Canada's North. How do you keep your guest's expectations in check?

A: Wildlife is scarce if the conditions aren't right: reduced food sources, reduced sea ice — even too much sea ice — bad weather. That is the challenge for us. We use the expertise of the people who have called the North home for thousands of years. They can read the ice, the land, and they understand the ways of the wildlife. Without their knowledge and experience, our job would be much harder.

Q: When's the best time of year to visit the ice floe, and why?

A: End of May into June, in the Arctic spring when the ice is still strong, but open water appears. That's when the marine mammals emerge.

Q: What's your favourite part of Canada's North?

A: If I have to pick one part of the Canadian North … I would pick Baffin Island. That is my home. I love the diversity of the landscape — from towering cliffs to tundra. From freshwater lakes to the sea-coast. Midnight sun or northern lights — Baffin Island delivers all the icons of the Canadian Arctic.

Q: Not everyone can join you for a hot air balloon over the ice floe. What belongs on everyone's Northern Canada Bucket List?

A: If you have a long weekend — Friday to Sunday — you can check the northern lights or the midnight sun off your bucket list. Iqaluit is only a three-hour direct flight from Ottawa. Stay for an extra night, and we can arrange to fly you to photograph wildlife or enjoy champagne on a glacier.

Q: Are there misconceptions about the North you want to clear up? I keep telling people that it does actually warm up in the summer!

A: Thank you for that … in mid-July some of our guests can be seen in T-shirts sunning themselves on our camp chairs! The Canadian Arctic is not an inferior Antarctica. The northern polar region is an ocean surrounded by land, whereas Antarctica is a continent surrounded by water. You can't say you are a polar traveller without having visited the Arctic.

Q: We've come a long way from the Franklin expedition. Is a northern expedition still considered dangerous?

A: Life in the North requires a greater attention to detail, perhaps, than southern Canada. Weather changes hourly. If the wind changes direction, the ice that had been floating away from land earlier could be driven back to shore. Our field team members are experienced and wise enough to rely on the advice of Inuit guides. We make sure our guests are fully briefed about visiting the North. We have been operating trips in the Arctic safely for nearly two decades. And we plan to continue to do that for many decades more.

WITNESS THE MIGRATION
OF THE OTHER BEAST

Just about everyone knows about the annual migration of the wilde-beest in East Africa. Indeed, the largest movement of land animals on the planet is on many a bucket list. The North has its own incredi-ble migration, although it is far less well-known. Every year, hundreds of thousands of caribou migrate across the Arctic. The Porcupine caribou herd migrate between Ivvavik National Park (page 7) and the Alaska Wildlife Reserve, while the Beverly and Qamanirjuaq herd migrate north to south on the Barren Lands west of Hudson Bay. Much like the great wildebeest trek between the Masai Mara and Serengeti, the sheer volume of one species attracts volumes of others. In the case of the Arctic, this includes some of the most elusive crea-tures on a wildlife lover's checklist: wolves and wolverines.

Arctic Haven is a remote lodge located at the treeline on the eighty-four-kilometre-long Ennadai Lake, one of the great lakes in Nunavut's Barren Lands region. Originally built as a remote fish-ing lodge, it was refashioned as a wildlife station in 2013, allowing visitors to finally witness the remarkable caribou migration. Each

spring and fall, up to three hundred thousand caribou migrate along the eskers and lakes of the Barren Lands, directly in the path of the post-and-beam lodge. There are activities for both warmer and cooler weather, including snowmobiling, dogsledding, tundra hiking, boating, kite skiing, and fishing for trophy-size lake trout, northern pike, and grayling. It's also a great spot to (finally) see the northern lights.

Ennadai Lake was the original home and hunting grounds of the Ahiarmiut people, who were forced to relocate by the government in 1949. Today, the lodge is partly owned by a pair of Nunavut entrepreneurs, and respect for the environment and landscape is impressive (the entire lodge is solar-powered). One doesn't expect gourmet meals, hot showers, wine, and wifi connections in the Arctic wilderness. Given the location, you can expect to pay what you would for a luxury safari lodge in the Serengeti. What you walk away with, on the other hand, is a one-of-a-kind wildlife and wilderness experience, guaranteed to blow the Tilley hat off of even the most experienced safari nut.

START HERE: canadianbucketlist.com/arctichaven

VISIT A NORSE GOD

Thor, the powerful god of Thunder (lately a hunky blond super-hero sharing screen time with the Hulk, Captain America, and Robert Downey Jr.) has traditionally wielded his mighty hammer in the mythical kingdom of Asgard. What if I were to tell you that both Thor and Asgard are located in a "land that never melts" right here in Canada? Auyuittuq was the first national park established in Nunavut, located on the east coast of Baffin Island. Carved by glaciers, some 85 percent of the park consists of rock and ice, a stark landscape that nevertheless attracts hikers and climbers from around

Sorry, Darling, England Needs Me

It was the most expensive stunt of its time, and perhaps the most daring opening sequence for a Bond film ever. In *The Spy Who Loved Me*, Roger Moore leaves a beautiful double-crossing blond agent in a remote ski cabin. Suddenly, half a dozen armed bad guys are chasing him in a thrilling ski chase, their bullets somehow missing Bond's eighties yellow jumpsuit. They corner him down on the edge of an enormous cliff. Bond skis right off the lip, the music pausing, along with our breaths, for a long twenty seconds. Finally, Bond opens a Union Jack parachute (of course), and the iconic James Bond theme kicks in on all cylinders. A close-up of Roger Moore, clearly against a studio backdrop, has him looking quite unperturbed. Stuntman Rick Sylvester successfully performed the ski/base jump stunt off Mount Asgard in what is now Auyuittuq National Park. Only James Bond can ski downhill for three minutes and arrive at the top of a mountain. ➤

the world. Each summer, with its proximity to Iqaluit, Auyuittuq becomes the most accessible park in Nunavut, and, therefore, its most affordable.

The star attraction is undoubtedly Thor Peak, the highest uninterrupted rock face on Planet Earth. Looming over the Weasel River Valley, Thor reduces its visitors to mere specks on the landscape. Mortals in the presence of a geological wonder, it is an awe-inspiring granite god of the natural world. If you hike farther along the Akshayuk Pass, you will stumble beneath the twin shadows of mighty Mount Asgard, two imposing cylindrical towers of granite separated by a saddle. If the God of Thunder existed beyond cartoon panels and summer blockbusters, Mount Asgard would be the perfect spot for him to live.

START HERE: canadianbucketlist.com/auyuittuq

EPILOGUE

My travels have allowed me to learn a thing or two: the importance of smiling and not panicking in tricky situations; trusting my instinct; keeping an open mind; remembering to check my expectations with my baggage. Perhaps the most important nugget of wisdom: it's the people we meet who create the paradise we find. Itineraries are an outline, but characters and personalities shade in the colours of any journey. My single biggest piece of advice when it comes to tackling any experience in this book is simple: share it with good people, and if you're on your own, be open and friendly to those around you.

It's also worth noting that travel is as personal as your choice of underwear. You might not meet the folks I met, have the same weather, or enjoy each experience as much as I did. Your experience of the North is as unique as yourself — even if you're only reading the pages of this book.

The Great Northern Canada Bucket List is a terrific start, but I'm well aware there are woeful omissions, items known and less known that I haven't got to just yet. Some of them will pop up on canadian-bucketlist.com, where you can also let me know what I'm missing. I expect my Canadian Bucket Lists will keep growing over the years, because the more we dig, the more we'll find, and the more we find, the more we can celebrate, sharing the best of Canada with locals and visitors alike. Rankin Inlet, ballooning above the floe edge, Wilberforce Falls — there's always more to discover. Every chapter in this book concludes with two important words: **START HERE**. I'll end the book with two more: **START NOW**.

RE
robin@robinesrock.com
@robinesrock

ACKNOWLEDGEMENTS

*T*he *Great Northern Canada Bucket List* is the result of many miles and many hours of travel, with the professional and personal help of many people and organizations. My deep gratitude to all below, along with all the wonderful folks I shared my adventures with.

YUKON: Travel Yukon, Jim Kemshead, Denny Kobayashi, Peter Mather, Marten Berkman, Frank Turner, Cyara Dodge, Parks Canada, Helena Katz, Guy Theriault, Peter Maher.

NORTHWEST TERRITORIES: Northwest Territories Tourism, Julie Warnock, Kyle Kisoun-Taylor, Barb Cote, Eva Holland, Tundra North Adventures, Carlos Gonzalez, Parks Canada.

NUNAVUT: One Ocean Expeditions, Aaron and Cathy Lawton, Elyse Mailhot, Jeff Topham, the staff, crew, and passengers of the *Akademik Sergey Vavilov*, Ryan Bray, Sara Acher, Richard Weber, Tessum Weber, Nansen Weber, Josee Auclair, and everyone at Arctic Watch, Ruslan Margolin, Prisca Campbell, Graham Dickson, Nunavut Tourism, Parks Canada.

SPECIAL THANKS: Karen McMullin, Margaret Bryant, Kirk Howard, Carrie Gleason, Allison Hirst, Laura Boyle, Synora van Drine, Courtney Horner, and all at Dundurn Press. Hilary McMahon and all at Westwood Creative Artists, Cathy Hirst and all at the Lavin Agency, Jon Rothbart, Joe Kalmek, David Rock, Guy Theriault, Leslie Qammaniq, Tamara Tarasoff, Paul Scriver, Heather Taylor, Jennifer Burnell, Cory Trépanier, Lauren More, Linda Bates, Patrick Crean, the Canadian Tourism Commission's

Go Media Marketplace, Josephine Wasch, Nathalie Gauthier, Kerri May, Jarrod Levitan, Vancouver and Burnaby Public Libraries, Chris Lee, Jeff Topham, Sherill Sirrs, Mary Rostad, RtCamp, and the Kalmek and Esrock families.

Thanks to everyone who has attended one of my speaking events and/or and registered on canadianbucketlist.com.

SPECIAL THANKS TO THE FOLLOWING, WITHOUT WHOM THERE WOULD BE NO COMPANION WEBSITE OR SPEAKING TOURS:

Ford Motors Canada, Parks Canada, VIA Rail, Travel Manitoba, Tourism Saskatchewan, Tourism New Brunswick, Great Canadian Trails, and Keen Footwear.

And finally, to my parents, Joe and Cheryl Kalmek (without whom there would be no Robin Esrock), my ever-supportive wife, Ana Carolina, and my daughter, Raquel Ayla. When in doubt, go north.

PHOTO CREDITS

OTHER GREAT BUCKET LIST ADVENTURE BOOKS

The Great Atlantic Canada Bucket List

Robin Esrock loves all that our eastern provinces have to offer, and so will you! Activities and destinations that might seem ho-hum to locals will amaze us "come-from-aways," whether we're driving on some of the world's most beautiful roads, catching some fresh seafood, hiking in the national parks, or discovering the region's storied history. *The Great Atlantic Canada Bucket List* highlights the best travel experiences to be had on Canada's East Coast.

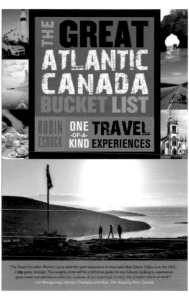

Not your typical travel guide, Robin's recommendations encompass outdoor adventure and natural wonders as well as the unique food, culture, and history of Canada's Atlantic Provinces.

Categorized by province, *The Great Atlantic Canada Bucket List* will give you a first-hand perspective on:

- Ziplining over a waterfall in New Brunswick.
- Harvesting an iceberg for a Newfoundland cocktail.
- Exploring Nova Scotia's Cabot Trail.
- Walking the seabed beneath Hopewell Rocks.
- Cycling across Prince Edward Island.
- Rafting a tidal wave in the Bay of Fundy.
- … and much more!

The Great Central Canada Bucket List

Most Canadians think of travel as a way to escape the snow, cold, and dreary winter skies. But Robin Esrock loves all that the provinces of Ontario and Quebec have to offer, and so will you! *The Great Central Canada Bucket List* highlights the best travel experiences to be had in the heart of Canada.

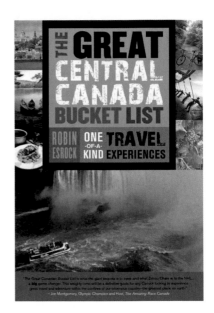

Renowned travel writer and TV host Robin Esrock explored every inch of central Canada to craft the definitive Bucket List for the region. Running the gamut of nature, food, culture, history, adrenaline rushes, and quirky Canadiana, Robin's personal quest to tick off the very best of Ontario and Quebec packs in enough for a lifetime.

Categorized by province, *The Great Central Canada Bucket List* will give you a first-hand perspective on:

- Riding a motorcycle around Lake Superior.
- Drinking *caribou* with Bonhomme.
- Unravelling a mystery in Algonquin Park.
- Spending the night at an ice hotel.
- Scaling the via ferrata at Mont-Tremblant.
- Exploring the great museums.
- Cave-swimming in the Magdalen Islands.
- … and much more!

The Great Canadian Prairies Bucket List

Robin Esrock was delighted to find Canada's Prairie Provinces have so much to offer both visitors and locals alike. Through his discovery of the local food, culture, history, natural beauty — and more than a few adrenaline rushes and some quirky tidbits of Canadiana — Robin's personal and often humorous quest to tick off the unique destinations and activities of the Prairies pack in enough adventure for a lifetime.

The Great Canadian Prairies Bucket List will give you a first-hand perspective on:

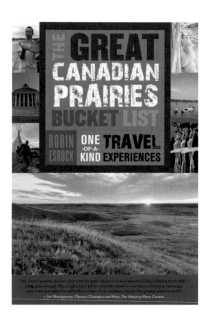

- Climbing Castle Butte in Big Muddy.
- Snorkelling with belugas.
- Exploring North America's largest sand dunes.
- Fishing for walleye and giant catfish.
- Cracking the mysterious Hermetic Code.
- Floating in Canada's very own Dead Sea.
- Tracking wolves in the snow.
- … and much more!

The Great Western Canada Bucket List

Most Canadians think of travel as a way to escape the snow, cold, and dreary winter skies. But Robin Esrock loves all that our western provinces have to offer, and so will you! *The Great Western Canada Bucket List* highlights some of the best travel experiences to be had on Canada's West Coast.

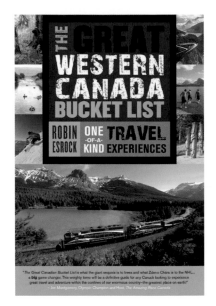

Through nature, food, culture, and history, as well as a few adrenaline rushes and some quirky Canadiana, Robin's personal quest to tick off the very best of Alberta and British Columbia packs in enough adventure for a lifetime.

Categorized by province, *The Great Western Canada Bucket List* will give you a first-hand perspective on:

- Sailing in Haida Gwaii.
- Tracking the spirit bear in B.C.'s Great Bear Rainforest.
- Wine-tasting in the Okanagan.
- Hunting for dinosaurs in Alberta's Badlands.
- Diving a sunken battleship.
- Snorkelling with salmon.
- Surviving the Calgary Stampede.
- RVing the Icefields Parkway.
- … and much more!

The Great Canadian Bucket List

Renowned travel writer and TV host Robin Esrock spent years visiting every province and territory to craft the definitive National Bucket List. Having travelled to more than one hundred countries on six continents, he never expected Canada to offer so much, and neither will you!

This isn't a typical travel guide — it is an inspiration for your next trip. Spanning the outdoors, food, culture, and history, Robin's personal journey to tick off the very best of Canada features well-known and hidden gems, and is infused with humour, trivia, advice, and unforgettable characters.

Categorized by province, *The Great Canadian Bucket List* will give you a first-hand perspective on:

- Tracking the Spirit Bear in BC's Great Bear Rainforest.
- Ziplining over a massive waterfall in New Brunswick.
- Digging for dinosaur bones in Alberta's Badlands.
- Harvesting an iceberg for a refreshing Newfoundland cocktail.
- Finding the best smoked meat sandwich in Montreal.
- Floating in Canada's very own Dead Sea.
- Cracking the nation's own Da Vinci Code in Winnipeg.
- Hiking the tundra under Nunavut's midnight sun.
- … and much more!

DUNDURN

VISIT US AT

Dundurn.com
@dundurnpress
Facebook.com/dundurnpress
Pinterest.com/dundurnpress